How to Meet the Right Man

How to Meet the Right Man

A Five-Step Strategy That Really Works

**Roger Ratcliff, David Conaway,
and Diana Ohlsson**

A Citadel Press Book
Published by Carol Publishing Group

Carol Publishing Group Edition, 1998

A Citadel Press Book
Published by Carol Publishing Group
Citadel Press is a registered trademark of Carol Communications, Inc.

Editorial, sales and distribution, and rights and permissions
inquiries should be addressed to Carol Publishing Group, 120
Enterprise Avenue, Secaucus, N.J. 07094

In Canada: Canadian Manda Group, One Atlantic Avenue, Suite 105,
Toronto, Ontario M6K 3E7

Carol Publishing Group books may be purchased in bulk at special
discounts for sales promotion, fund-raising, or educational
purposes. Special editions can be created to specifications. For
details, contact Special Sales Department, Carol Publishing Group,
120 Enterprise Avenue, Secaucus, N.J. 07094

Manufactured in the United States of America
10 9 8 7 6 5 4 3 2 1

Library of Congress Cataloging-in-Publication Data
Ratcliff, Roger.
    How to meet the right man : a five-step strategy that really
works / Roger Ratcliff, David Conaway, and Diana Ohlsson.
        p.   cm.
    "A Citadel Press book."
    ISBN 0-8065-2016-7 (pbk.)
    1. Mate selection   2. Man-woman relationships.   3. Dating (Social
customs)   I. Conaway, David.   II. Ohlsson, Diana.   III. Title.
HQ801.R258   1996
646.7'7—dc20   96-33581
                                                              CIP

Contents

❧Introduction❧
How to Meet Mr. Right

*T*his book is based on a class we teach on how to meet the opposite sex. After teaching hundreds of men and women of all ages (and seeing their many successes), we know that our methods can help you with the important, and sometimes difficult, challenge of finding a love partner. We teach an organized approach that will enable you to take control of your own destiny and avoid the frustration of waiting either for your friends to fix you up or for a chance encounter with a desirable man.

This book is for you if:

♦ You have been unable to find a man who is truly right for you.
♦ You are tired of men judging you only on your looks.
♦ You have been meeting nothing but jerks.
♦ You have stayed in relationships only because they were "better than nothing."
♦ Your present method for meeting men has not produced the results you desire.
♦ You want a proven method that will bring success.

While there are dozens of "How to Meet a Man" books, most of them concentrate on the psychological issues of getting ready for a new relationship and having a good relationship. They have little to say about how to meet a man and arrange the first date—something that obviously must be accomplished before *any* relationship can begin. Our book fills the niche left by the relationship books already on the market by teaching the skills needed to meet a desirable man and arrange that critical first date.

There are skills you can learn and actions you can take, some amazingly simple, that will greatly increase your chances of meeting a man who will be right for you.

Jill, a friend of ours who took our class and then put our methods into practice, had this to say about how the class changed her outlook:

> I like the feeling of walking into a place and knowing how to meet any man I choose; and that's not because I'm so great looking—I'm not. It's only because I have learned the basic steps. Whether it's a singles event, a supermarket, or a lecture, I know what to do to make myself more approachable, and when I see a man who really interests me, I know subtle ways to take the initiative to meet him. The men have no idea what I'm doing.
>
> I have been on the other side of the fence—not having a clue as to what to do—and it's no fun. Before I learned the simple steps needed to meet a man, I would go out to try to meet someone, but when I got there I wouldn't know what to do or say and I would feel self-conscious and uncomfortable. It wasn't a situation I liked being in. And going home without even having talked to a man didn't make me want to go out again.
>
> Knowing the basics makes all the difference. I'm meeting men now and getting dates. I no longer go home with a frustrated and hopeless feeling like I used to. Going out looking is actually becoming exciting. Even though I haven't found my man yet, I'm having fun while I look. I know it's only a matter of time now.

You don't have to be "without a clue" when it comes to meeting men. Like Jill, you can learn simple, fundamental methods that don't depend on luck. We have put our highly effective, commonsense methods into an easy-to-learn format.

Three of us have written this book: Dave, Roger, and Diana. All of us have faced the real-world problems of meeting someone and have learned the skills necessary to be successful. With this book, you can also learn these skills.

All of the stories in this book are true. Names have been changed for the usual reasons.

DAVE AND ROGER'S STORY

How did we begin teaching women how to meet men? It took quite a while—years in fact. Both of our marriages ended at about the same time, and we both found ourselves in our forties and without a clue as to how to meet women. Because we worked in the same building, we were able to meet for lunch several times a week. Our favorite topic at these lunchtime bull sessions was how men and women meet. As you would expect from two aerospace engineers, we analyzed the meeting process to death. We spent hundreds of hours discussing why some techniques work better than others, where to go to meet people, and why people are so held back by their fear of rejection.

Whenever one of us was out of a relationship and looking again, we had an opportunity to test our theories. Over the years, we developed a good understanding of the fundamentals of meeting for romance and considerable expertise at putting this understanding into practice. We began to wonder if anyone in the world had analyzed the subject of how to meet for romance more than we had. We joked that we knew enough to write a book or teach a class on this subject, and four years ago, on a lark, we did start teaching a class for men called "Meeting Women Made Easy." Preparing for this class forced us to organize our techniques into an easy-to-learn format.

After teaching this class for several months, we began to realize that we also had a lot to teach women about how to meet *men*. Men in our class often complained that women don't do anything to help men meet them—they leave it all up to the man. One man even went so far as to say, "Sometimes women who appear to be trying to meet someone actually do things that make it harder to approach them." We agreed with these observations. It seems that most women don't understand men's deep-seated fear of approaching women. We knew we could help women be more approachable by teaching them methods to reduce men's fear. We also knew we could teach women the same active technique we were teaching men, an effective technique few women use.

With the encouragement of some female friends, we started teaching a class for women called "Meeting Men Made Easy." In this class some women complained that they weren't being approached by men. We taught these women a technique that doesn't depend exclusively on their looks. Other women said they were approached a lot, but the men they were meeting always turned out to be jerks. We taught *these* women a technique for learning more about a man before they agreed to a date, as well as a way to meet a different kind of man, a man less likely to be a jerk.

We became acquainted with Diana when she was a student in one of our early classes. She was very enthusiastic about our approach and ultimately was a great help in providing a woman's perspective. (Read on for her story.)

Eventually we combined the men's and women's classes into one class. We have taught hundreds of men and women ranging in age from teenagers to retirees. Some wanted to learn how to meet the opposite sex so they could get married and raise a family, others just wanted companionship. High school and college students, blue-collar workers, white-collar workers, and professionals have all found our class helpful. The many success stories we hear from our students validate our methods. In this book we use their stories and ours, along with tips and diagrams, to help you gain an in-depth understanding of important techniques and concepts.

During one of our classes, a woman said, "Your method for meeting men doesn't sound very romantic." We agreed with her 100 percent. There is nothing romantic about our method whatsoever. We get the myths and misconceptions out of the way and teach a method that is effective. The romance starts when you go out on your first date with an appealing man. We teach the fundamentals of the meeting process so you can find that man and get that first date.

DIANA'S STORY

When I was married I had always assumed that I was going to spend the rest of my life with my husband. But he wanted out. The divorce was devastating. For a long time afterward I was lonely and had low self-esteem. I felt totally lost because I didn't know where to go or what to do or say to meet men. Since I wasn't meeting *any* men, it seemed pretty hopeless that I would ever find a good man whom I would love and who would love me in return. After spending most of my adult life married, I wasn't prepared for the singles world that I faced, and the fact that my fortieth birthday was coming up didn't help my outlook one bit.

That was my state of mind when I signed up for Dave and Roger's class, "Meeting Men Made Easy." The straightforward and useful advice they gave in that class turned out to be exactly what I needed. They made me realize that there was hope for me after all. Although at that time I felt that I didn't have the nerve to do everything they recommended, at least I finally knew what needed to be done—I had some direction.

I stayed after the class to talk with Dave and Roger. They seemed genuinely interested in the problems I was having meeting men, and they welcomed my comments on their class. Because it was late, they suggested that I meet them for dinner the next day to continue our discussion. I think Dave and Roger had an ulterior motive when they extended their dinner invitation: They wanted to get a woman's in-depth opinion on what they were teaching. I *also* had an ulterior motive: I wanted more help with my problem of finding a good man.

Our dinner conversation turned out to be mutually beneficial, and dinner together became a regular event. Later, after I had become adept at using the techniques for meeting men that they had taught me, I started helping them teach their classes. Eventually I helped them write this book, as well as our companion book, *How to Meet the Right Woman*.

The problems I faced in those first years after my divorce are faced by many women. The combination of the devastation of the divorce, the loneliness, the lack of confidence, and the hopelessness of not knowing how to meet a good man was almost too much to bear. As I began using the techniques for meeting men that are in this book, I came to realize how interrelated all these problems really were. Even a little success in the "meeting a man" arena gave me tremendous hope, improved my outlook, and helped in the "recovering from divorce" arena. Few things will do more for your self-confidence than knowing that you have the ability to meet, and sometimes date, an interesting, appealing man.

Without the advice that Dave and Roger gave me, my recovery would have been much slower. With no success in meeting men, I don't know if I would have ever regained my self-confidence. Without any hope, I might have ended up like some women I know who have simply given up. They have little hope; they put little effort into trying to find a man, and they are, for the most part, unhappy with the state of their love lives.

I'm not married yet, and marriage is still my goal; however, right now I am involved with a wonderful guy. We have a lot in common and the future looks good. If this doesn't work out, I will be disappointed, but I won't be devastated because I now have the know-how to meet another man. I have faith in my ability to influence my destiny, and what I want is to be married to the right guy.

Whatever your situation is—whether you are staying in an unsatisfying relationship because you think it is either that man or none; whether you are newly divorced or just broken up with your boyfriend; whether you are meeting few men, or meeting few *good* men—this book can help you. Following its advice will help you bring the right man into your life.

Part I

Empowering Yourself With the Facts

1

The Passive Technique
How to Be More Approachable

few weeks after coming out of a troubled relationship, Donna came to us for some tips on how to meet guys. We recommended that she go to the party at the Grand Hotel on Friday evening. The previous year this event, which was billed as "The World's Largest Office Party," had attracted nearly a thousand singles, with noticeably more men than women.

Donna went to the party with her girlfriends and had a disappointing evening. When she checked back with us, she said, "No, I didn't meet anybody. I stood there all evening and a lot of men saw me, but they never came over to talk. Is there something wrong with me? I had on slacks and most of the women wore dresses. Could that be it?"

Donna assumed she wasn't approached because there was something about her looks that men didn't like. That could be true. One big reason a man won't approach a woman is that he doesn't like her looks. In Donna's case, however, we felt it was the other big reason, and that is:

MOST MEN ARE AFRAID TO APPROACH WOMEN!

That's right! Football jocks, accountants, executives, college men, and young and old men from all walks of life are afraid to approach women. The majority of men in our class listed "fear of approaching women" as their biggest problem in getting a date.

One of these men, Dan, described the effect this fear has on him:

One night as I was leaving a wine-tasting party, I analyzed what I was doing wrong. There must have been two hundred women there, and I hadn't gotten into a conversation with a single one. It finally dawned on me what my problem was. I would always divide the women into two groups. One group was the women I didn't want to meet. The other group was the women I found appealing, but was afraid to approach because I assumed they didn't want to meet me. I was spending my time looking for a woman who somehow fell in the middle, a woman I wanted to meet and who I assumed would also want to meet me. But no one ever fit that description. As soon as I became interested in a woman she would automatically go into the category of women who I assumed wouldn't want me, and I would be afraid to approach her.

When you wait for the man to take the initiative, you are using what we call the "Passive Technique." To be more successful with the Passive Technique, consider the man's fear and do whatever you can to make it easier for him to approach you. When a man sees you and is interested in meeting you, consciously or unconsciously he asks himself several questions:

Is she single?
Does she look as if she wants to meet me?
How easy will it be to get near her?
What can I say to start a conversation?
How easy will it be to ask her out?
Will I be rejected?

A man will decide whether or not to approach you based on his answers to those questions. Your behavior can influence his decision. Here's how to make yourself more approachable.

Be Alone

Being with a group of women greatly reduces your chances of meeting a man. At least 90 percent of our male students say they prefer to approach a woman who is alone. Here are some of their reasons:

"I won't approach a woman who is in a group. I don't need an audience when I get shot down. I don't want half the universe watching."

"I have trouble enough starting a conversation with one woman; with two or more it's impossible."

"How do I let one woman know I like her and not her girlfriends?"

"How am I supposed to ask a woman out in front of her friends? 'Mary, could we meet for lunch tomorrow? I'm not interested in the rest of you.' "

If you go out with other women for safety or moral support, separate when you get to an event. Meet occasionally to exchange notes, but be alone most of the time. Kristy, a student of ours, describes how going out alone affected her personality:

I used to go to singles dances with my girlfriend, and I would spend most of the evening talking to her. If she couldn't go, I would stay home. After I took your class, I got up my nerve and tried going to these dances without her. The first time I went alone I thought, "If it's going to happen, it's up to me." Not having my friend to use as a crutch changed my personality. I became more outgoing and talked to more men. Besides that, I noticed that when I was alone I was approached more often. Now I always go alone.

Women who aren't used to being alone in singles places often have strong negative reactions to the idea. For example, here are some of the comments we heard from women in our class:

"I'd feel sleazy going out alone."

"I'd feel like a slut being at a singles bar alone."

"I'm afraid to go out alone."

The first time we heard a woman say that being out alone made her feel like a slut, we were surprised. We have been to many singles meeting places and have never felt that a woman's character was in any way determined by whether she was alone or with a group. Most men in our class agree with us on this issue.

For example, here is what Mike had to say:

I think it's silly to say that a woman who is out alone is in any way sleazy. When I'm at a singles event, if I see a woman by herself, I get interested because I know it's easier to talk to a woman who is alone, and it's a whole lot easier to ask her out.

Few men make negative assumptions about a woman's character because she is alone. Besides, when a man sees you alone, he doesn't really know that you are alone. You may be waiting for a friend to arrive or for one to return from the restroom, buffet, or dance floor.

Be Visible and Accessible

Position yourself where you can be easily seen and easily approached. Obviously, before a man can decide to approach you, he must know that you are there. Once he has seen you, however, if he can't easily get near you to start a conversation, he may chicken out.

At some events you can be both visible and accessible by positioning yourself near a high-traffic area where men will pass by. Men can then see you and easily get near you. For example, if you are near the path to a dance floor or restroom, it is easier for men because they can head in your direction without feeling obvious. They may even pass by several times before getting up the nerve to stop and talk. Or you can linger by the buffet table where a man can get near you by pretending he's interested in the food. Once he is near, a comment about the buffet gives him an easy way to start a conversation.

If there is a crowd of people, stay on the fringes where you are highly visible. You will then be in a position where a man can easily work his way over and then "just happen" to be standing beside you.

Standing is usually better than sitting because you are more accessible to men who want to start a conversation. A man can easily stand next to you and say something. When you sit in a low chair, a man will either have to look down as he speaks, bend over, or kneel on the floor next to your chair. Most men don't like speaking to a woman from any of these positions.

If you do sit, it's best to sit on something high, such as a bar stool, where a man can stand next to you, make eye contact, and casually begin a conversation. In a group of tables, select a table near the outer edge where you can be easily seen and take a chair on the side of the table where men will be passing by. Avoid any seat where a man would have to weave between the tables in order to approach you. Few things make a man feel more conspicuous than this type of approach.

Make Eye Contact and Smile

If an intriguing man looks your way, smile and meet his gaze for a moment before looking away. If he smiles or keeps returning your glances, make it easy for him to approach. If you are with other people, break off from the group. Go to the bar, buffet table, or drinking fountain where he has an excuse to be near you or make a quick trip to the restroom. Make eye contact and smile as you pass by him on your way there and returning. Your smile will encourage him to meet you because it shows you are interested.

Wear or Carry a Conversation Piece

A man may want to meet you but be reluctant to approach because he doesn't know what to say to start a conversation. When you wear or carry something he can comment on, you give him an idea for an icebreaker. Here are some suggestions for conversation pieces that will give him something to ask a question about or compliment you on:

♦ Wear a button that has words or a picture.

♦ Wear a T-shirt or sweatshirt that has words or a picture.

♦ Wear a prominent and unusual piece of jewelry.

♦ Wear something flashy, such as a bright scarf.

♦ Wear a jaunty hat or cap.

♦ Carry an unusual purse.

♦ Carry a book that has an interesting or provocative title.

Jason's story shows how a conversation piece can give a man an opener.

I was at the airport waiting for my flight when I noticed a woman I wanted to meet. She was alone, and looked as if she might be on the same flight. I wanted to talk to her, but I was at a loss for words until I noticed a large button on her sweater which said, "Be a Panda Pal." I walked up to her and said, "So what's a Panda Pal?" That's all it took. She was a supporter of a wildlife organization and loved talking about it. If she wasn't wearing that button, I probably wouldn't have met her.

It's not easy for a man to think of an opener when he's near a woman he would like to meet. Give him some help—wear a conversation piece. More men will speak to you when they have an easy opener.

Don't Wear a Ring on Your Wedding-Ring Finger

A woman in a singles bar was sitting alone. On her wedding-ring finger she was wearing the traditional ring that screams out to men, "This woman is married!" A man standing nearby noticed the ring and said, "Excuse me—are you married?"

"No, I'm not."

"Why are you wearing a wedding ring?"

"This ring was a gift from my daughter."

"Why are you wearing it on your wedding-ring finger?"

"What finger do you expect me to wear it on? That's the only one it fits."

Her reply was mind-boggling. She was in a singles bar and looked as if she were trying to meet a man, yet she was wearing a traditional wedding ring. Many men would assume she was married and not approach her.

Men usually check for a wedding ring. From across a room, it's difficult to tell what kind of ring a woman is wearing. A man looking for an excuse to avoid facing rejection often assumes *any* ring on the left-hand ring finger is a wedding ring. To avoid a misinterpretation, don't wear a ring of any kind on that finger.

These suggestions for making yourself more approachable can make a big difference. Don't underestimate their power. Most men are afraid to approach women, and anything you do to reduce their fear will help. If you follow these suggestions, you will increase your chances of success. In the next chapter, however, we will teach you a technique for meeting men that will bring you even more success.

The Active Technique

The Most Effective Way to Meet a Man

The Active Technique in which you approach a man, start a conversation, and ask for a date is much better than the traditional Passive Technique of waiting for a man to approach you. The Active Technique is by far the most effective way to meet a man.

Denise is a thirty-nine-year-old legal secretary. After her divorce, she hoped to meet a compatible man, but there were no available men where she worked, and her friends didn't know any eligible men. After a year without a date, Denise realized she was going to have to go out and find a man. Here is her story.

After my divorce my busy schedule made it hard for me to meet men. My two daughters took a lot of my time, and I rode the bus to work downtown, making for a long day. I was also getting an M.B.A. at night school, and that meant most evenings I was either in class or studying. Saturday night was my only chance to get out, and I always went to the dance put on by a singles group. I was comfortable there. It didn't seem as threatening as the singles bars.

At first, I always sat at a table in the corner. That didn't work. Nobody ever came over and asked me to dance. Then my girlfriend said, "You have to sit here at the bar and face the dance floor like this." She turned around on her bar stool, leaned back against the bar, and crossed her legs, showing some thigh. When I protested, "I can't do that!" she insisted, "Yes, you can! This is what you *have* to do." I tried her method and she was right. More men talked to me and more men asked me to dance. Then I discovered it was better to stand by the edge of the dance floor. Later I learned it was better to move around through the crowd. One man commented, "You move like a man. I've watched you go from corner to corner." I knew what he meant and took it as a compliment. Next I discovered it was better to pick the man I wanted to meet and ask him to dance. Sitting around waiting to be approached doesn't work for me.

Denise's switch from the Passive to the Active Technique didn't occur overnight. It took going to that Saturday night dance for nearly a year before she was comfortable in the active role. If she had been able to get out more than once a week, she would have improved that much faster. Using the Active Technique, Denise met and started dating Kurt. Here is Kurt's description of their first meeting:

I noticed Denise early in the evening, but I didn't ask her to dance because I didn't find her attractive. However, when I was resting between dances she came over to me and said, "I was watching you dance. You're a great dancer. Would you dance with me?"

I know what it feels like to be turned down, so on the rare occasion when a woman asks me to dance, I always dance at least one number. But while I was having what I thought was my one dance with Denise, I found out she was a lot of fun. Pretty soon we were dancing real close and doing a lot of kidding around. I remember asking her how long she thought it would be before I kissed her. She replied, "Certainly not on the first date." With that, I leaned down and kissed her cheek and we both laughed at my little joke. Although it was still early in the evening, I knew I wanted to see her again, so I asked her if she would like to go somewhere and get some dessert. She accepted my invitation, and we were out the door.

Denise's looks were not enough to make Kurt want to know her, but when she gave him a chance to see her personality, he liked her and asked her out. If Denise had depended on the Passive Technique, she wouldn't have met Kurt.

ADVANTAGES OF THE ACTIVE TECHNIQUE

Advantage No. 1: You Have a Larger Selection of Men

When you use the Passive Technique you can select only from the men who approach *you*. This is usually a small percentage of the men at an event, and sometimes none at all. With the Active Technique, you can select from all the men there. Men traditionally select from all the women at an event. Why should you be satisfied selecting from just the men who approach you?

Advantage No. 2: Men Can Judge Your Personality, Not Just Your Looks

If you use the Passive Technique, men must judge you solely on your looks. If you use the Active Technique, you allow a man to also see your personality.

Beautiful women are sometimes puzzled that a woman would ever want to use the Active Technique. At a party, as we were describing the Active Technique to Mary, she looked increasingly agitated. She finally had to tell us her opinion of the Active Technique. She said, "It's not necessary for women to do that at all. They should just go out, have a good time, and let the men come up to them. That's all it takes. Why just the other day I went to a volleyball game and screamed and jumped around, and three men asked me out."

There was no doubt Mary could get dates without taking the initiative to approach men; she was extremely attractive. Some women are so attractive they don't even have to go out to meet men. When asked where she went to meet men, another beautiful woman at the party replied, "I don't go anywhere. Men come up to me on the street, in the supermarket, at work—wherever I am. My last boyfriend stopped me on the street and asked for directions, then he asked me out. I never go out to meet men."

Unfortunately, not every woman is blessed with such beauty that men are constantly asking her out. One woman remarked, "Men used to come up to me, but now they don't. I have reached an age where men look right through me. My girlfriends tell me I should just give up and start doing more things with them. I guess I'm supposed to recede now and become wallpaper."

The bottom line is, if you want men to judge you on your personality, not just your looks, take the initiative—use the Active Technique.

Advantage No. 3: You Meet Men Who May Be More Desirable

Even if you effortlessly attract men, there is still a reason to use the Active Technique: You can meet a different kind of man—quite possibly a more desirable man. Beth, an attractive student of ours, complained that she had trouble keeping relationships going. When asked how she met men, Beth said she always used the Passive Technique. She told the class, "When I go out to meet men, I usually sit in an inaccessible spot. That way I figure that any man who comes up to me really wants me. I want a man who really wants me."

Beth's understanding of why men approach her is wrong. The men who approach an attractive woman like Beth in an inaccessible spot are the ones who have the nerve to do so; they don't necessarily want her more than the other men there. In fact, the men who don't approach her may want her more, but lack the nerve to try to meet her. Beth's technique results in her meeting the "experts," men skilled at meeting women. The experts, as many women have learned, are not necessarily the most desirable men for a long-term relationship. This might account for Beth's relationship problems.

At a typical singles event the experts will be meeting and talking to

All the Men at an Event

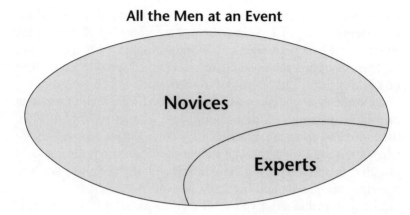

women. The majority of men, however, the novices, will be standing alone or talking to other men. One woman described these inactive men as "the gray faces lining the walls." The figure above represents all the men at an event. Normally, there are far more novices.

Tony, a handsome student in one of our classes, is a good example of an expert. As Tony described his methods for meeting women, we began to realize this was something he was good at. We couldn't understand why such a Don Juan would sign up for a class on how to get a date. He must have felt that meeting women was a subject you could never know too much about. A few months later, when asked if our class had been of any help, Tony eagerly explained how his results had improved:

> Oh yes! Your class helped me a lot. Before I took your class I was getting about fifteen numbers a month. Now I'm getting closer to thirty. And since you told me it's not necessary to buy a woman a drink before asking for her number, I'm saving money, too. But I almost never call them. When I think about them the next day, they never seem as great as they did the night before. Besides, I already have a girlfriend.

Tony's story illustrates a potential problem with the experts: They might not treat you very well. Like Tony, they might take your number and not call, they might date several women at once, or they might end a relationship because of a minor disagreement. The expert's ability to get dates can make him hard to hang on to. Women in our class often complain that they are meeting nothing but jerks. Perhaps these women are meeting the experts.

With the Passive Technique you are most likely to meet the experts—men experienced enough to come up to you and ask you for a date. Back among those novices lining the walls, however, are many worthwhile men who lack the nerve or skill to meet women. If you use the Active Technique and take the initiative to meet a man from this group, you may get a man who doesn't meet many women and who is eager to have a woman in his life. A novice may be more likely to appreciate you and ride out rough spots in a relationship.

Advantage No. 4: You Gain Control

In one of our classes we asked the women how many of them waited for a man to take the initiative. Every woman raised her hand. We then asked them what they usually do when first arriving at a singles event. Sharon replied, "The first thing I do is check out the other women to see what the competition is like." The men in the class were caught off guard by her answer. Men rarely think about checking out the other men at singles events. Most men are too busy checking out the women. This shows the difference in thinking between the Passive and the Active Techniques. When you use the Active Technique, the man you meet is determined by which man you approach, not by what the other women look like.

Another woman in our class said, "I really dread being at a dance and standing there wondering who is going to ask me to dance. So often it's some big sweaty guy I don't want to meet, and I wind up dancing with him just to be nice. Then the next thing I know he wants to dance real close, or he wants to dance all night, or he asks me out. The whole thing is terrible." Avoid this situation by using the Active Technique. With the Active Technique you select the men you want to meet. You are not limited to just those who approach you. The Active Technique puts you, not the men, in control.

In summary, the Active Technique is significantly more effective than the Passive Technique. If men are not approaching you, use the

Active Technique to let them see your personality, not just your appearance. If men are approaching you, but you are meeting only jerks, use the Active Technique to meet a different kind of man—a man from the novice group. You are more likely to be appreciated and treated well by a novice than by an expert.

ACTIVE TECHNIQUE SUCCESS STORIES

Beth, a thirty-year-old chemist, tells how she met her husband:

> I always felt that any man I married would have to like stren-uous outdoor activities because that's such a big part of my life. I used to meet men roller blading downtown. I also joined the Mountain Club. That's where I met Andy.
>
> The Mountain Club puts on hikes that are graded accord-ing to their level of difficulty. I started out in the easy A-level hikes, but they weren't for me. There were more women than men, and the hikes were too slow. I progressed through the B- and C-level hikes and kept on going until I was doing techni-cal climbing; you know, rope, ice axe—that sort of thing. I was often the lone female on those climbs.
>
> On one technical climb I was on the rope just below Andy. I was trying to talk to Andy while this guy below me was hint-ing around that he would like to take me out, but he didn't come right out and ask for a date. Andy was taking it all in. I asked Andy what he and his wife had planned for that evening, and he said he wasn't married. Then I asked him if he got along with his ex, and he said he had never been married. This both-ered me because I thought he looked about forty, and if he had gone that long without getting married, what were my chances?
>
> When we finished the climb and were back at the cars, I asked Andy, "Would you like to trade numbers in case one of us needs a climbing partner someday?" I was pretty excited when Andy agreed to trade numbers, because I really liked him and I expected him to call. But a week went by and he didn't call. I got tired of waiting, so I got up my nerve and called him

and asked if he would like to go climbing with me on the weekend. He accepted, we had a great climb together, and then the next week he called me and suggested we go climbing.

The first time I called Andy it took a lot of nerve, but I'm glad I did it. Now we are married, and climbing is still a big part of our lives.

Beth's story confirms that women don't have to wait for luck (or men) to change their lives. Beth joined a club where there were lots of men who shared her interest in hiking and climbing. She selected the man she wanted to meet, got his telephone number, and called him. Perhaps Andy was too shy to take the initiative, or perhaps he didn't really start liking Beth until he got to know her better. Whatever the case, Beth took the initiative, and it resulted in marriage. She is proud of her accomplishment.

Linda is another woman who had success with the Active Technique. She recently married Burt, who is outgoing and talkative around men, but shy around women. If Linda hadn't taken the initiative to begin their relationship, they both might still be alone. Here is her story:

Burt and I had been working in the same group for over a year. I knew he wasn't dating anyone, and I kept hoping he would ask me out, but he never did. However, when Burt found out I was changing apartments, he offered to help me move and volunteered the use of his truck.

We were together all that day, and I thought it was the beginning of a relationship. But after the move, he didn't call, so I thought of a way I could ask him out. I invited him over for dinner to thank him for helping me move. He came to dinner and seemed to enjoy the evening, but he still didn't call or ask me out. I was beginning to think he wasn't interested in me, but I decided to try one more time. I asked him if he would like to take a bike ride on the weekend. He agreed to go, and that did the trick. Burt finally got the message that I liked him and we started dating.

Here is how Burt viewed their early involvement:

I had always wanted to date Linda, but I didn't think she would go out with me. I felt that she could have any man she wanted, and I couldn't imagine her wanting me. I didn't date in high school or college, and I had zero confidence when it came to asking women out. When I heard that Linda needed help moving, I was glad to help her. I wasn't surprised that she was willing to use my truck and let me help her move. After all, it saved her a lot of work and some money, too. And when she invited me to dinner to thank me, I didn't consider it a date; I assumed she felt obligated. It was only when she asked me to go on a bike ride that it finally dawned on me that she might be interested in me.

Burt worked with Linda and liked both her looks and personality, but he didn't ask her out because he was shy and inexperienced at dating. If Linda hadn't used the Active Technique, she and Burt might not be married today. Nothing subtle would have worked with Burt, certainly not the Passive Technique. Linda had to do all of the inviting until Burt was finally assured he was wanted.

MEN DON'T LIKE AGGRESSIVE WOMEN: A MYTH

When we recommend the Active Technique to the women in our class, they often protest, "But men don't like aggressive women." Perhaps some men don't like aggressive women in other areas of life, but in the meeting process, most men are pleased and flattered when approached by a woman. Surveys taken in our class show the vast majority of men would like to be approached by a woman they would like to meet. Most men say they would find it a pleasant surprise.

Jessica, one of our students who switched from the Passive to the Active Technique, told of an experience she had that debunked the aggressive-woman myth:

I was talking to a handsome, athletic-looking man who I later learned was an executive for a large corporation. I sensed that he liked me, but he didn't ask me out, so I asked him out instead. He accepted, and expressed surprise that I had asked him for a date. We kept talking for a while, and when the conversation drifted back to the subject of women asking men out, he said, "I can't imagine a man turning down a woman who asks for a date. When you asked me out, I was flattered. That has never happened to me before."

If you attempt to meet a man and are rejected, don't attribute the rejection to the myth that men don't like aggressive women. The rejection only means that for any number of reasons, the man isn't interested in meeting you. He might be gay, he might be in a relationship, or you might not be his type of woman. You will seldom be rejected by a man simply because you are actively trying to meet him. Many meeting opportunities are missed because the man is afraid to take the initiative. With the Active Technique, you can turn missed opportunities into meeting opportunities.

3

The Five Steps

$\mathcal{A}$s you learned in the previous chapter, the Active Technique has these advantages over the Passive Technique:

♦ You have a larger selection of men.
♦ Men can judge your personality, not just your looks.
♦ You meet men who may be more desirable.
♦ You gain control.

Unfortunately, there is a downside: The Active Technique is scary. Approaching a stranger and starting a conversation is not easy for most people. To make it less frightening, we have broken the Active Technique into five sequential steps. Viewing the process this way allows you to face only one step at a time. It can be frightening to think, "I have to go over there, talk with that man, and get a date." It's much less threatening to think, "I have to get near that man."

Each of the Five Steps that you complete increases your chances of success. You won't always have to complete all the steps. Sometimes, after you have executed two or three steps, the man will complete the remaining steps. Let's look at an example of how a woman might use the Active Technique in an adult enrichment class. We will then break the process into a series of small steps.

Nancy signed up for the course "Where Do All the Singles Go?" She assumed that most of the men in this class would be unattached and open to a relationship. The class was scheduled for a Saturday morning from nine to twelve. Nancy arrived for the class early, but before going in, she drove around the neighborhood looking for a place to have lunch after class. She found a Greek bakery nearby that had an outdoor eating area; just the type of place she had been looking for.

Nancy was the first student to arrive for class. She had her choice of places to sit, but she didn't take a seat or reserve a chair by hanging her jacket on it. Instead, she remained standing and read the bulletin board while waiting for the other students to arrive. As each man entered the room, she greeted him with a smile. Her plan was to select an interesting-looking man and sit beside him.

As people took their seats, they would leave an empty chair or so between themselves and those already seated. This typical behavior of giving others their personal space would enable Nancy to sit beside the man she wanted to meet.

Several men arrived, but Nancy continued to wait. Her patience paid off when a man who seemed interesting arrived and returned her smile. As predicted, he took a seat next to an empty chair. At this critical moment, Nancy hesitated as she thought, "He's going to know what I'm doing." She knew, however, that if she waited, another woman might sit next to him; then she would have to spend the entire class watching as *her* man flirted and joked with another woman.

Gathering her courage, Nancy sat beside him and said, "Hi! Have you heard anything about the instructor?" After a brief chat about the instructor and the class, Nancy introduced herself and learned that her classmate's name was Gary.

During the morning break, they continued their conversation. Nancy asked what he did for a living and where he worked. Gary said he was a C.P.A. and worked for Carson, Pratt and Company. As the break was ending, Nancy said, "I know a little Greek bakery over on Temple Street that has an outdoor eating area. I was thinking about stopping there after class for a bite to eat. Would you like to join me?" Gary broke into a big smile and agreed to join her for lunch. After class, Gary followed Nancy to the Greek bakery in his car.

During lunch, Nancy asked him what he liked to do for fun. She learned that he liked bike riding and was eager to try out his new mountain bike. Nancy said that she, too, had a mountain bike and mentioned a few of her favorite places to ride.

Nancy thought lunch went well. She wanted to see Gary again and felt that he liked her. As they walked to their cars after lunch, however, Gary didn't ask her out. Therefore, before she got in her car, she said, "I enjoyed having lunch with you. You know, it might be fun to take a bike ride together sometime. Here's my card. My work number is on there. Give me a call if you want to go for a ride." Gary accepted the card, read it quickly, and thanked her. On Monday, he called Nancy and made a date for a bike ride.

Here are the Five Steps Nancy took that resulted in her getting a date with Gary:

Step 1—Search

Nancy's search strategy was to wait near the door and watch the men entering the classroom.

Step 2—Get Near

Nancy got near the man she wanted to meet by taking the seat next to him. The instant she took that seat, she became the woman in the class most likely to meet him. This one action dramatically increased her chances of success. If Nancy had taken a seat when she first arrived, she would not have been able to choose which man she was going to sit beside for the class.

Step 3—Break the Ice

Nancy began a conversation with the simple icebreaker, "Have you heard anything about the instructor?"

Step 4—Continue the Conversation

Nancy kept the initial conversation going by talking about the instructor and the class. During the break she asked Gary personal questions that kept the conversation rolling and gave her important information about him. Nancy's invitation for Gary to join her for lunch extended their time together, giving her a chance to learn more about him. During lunch, when Nancy said she had a mountain bike and loved to ride, she provided Gary with an opportunity to ask her out. Unfortunately, her hint received no response.

Step 5—Close

As they parted, Nancy suggested they go on a bike ride and gave Gary her number. She assumed that he would call if he liked her since he already knew she wanted to go out and had her number. If Gary didn't call, Nancy had a backup plan. She would call Gary at work and invite him to join her for a bike ride. She thought she could reach him again because she knew his first name, the name of his company, and his job title. Nancy didn't want to use this bold approach, however, unless it was absolutely necessary. She wanted to first give Gary every chance to ask her out.

The way that Nancy applied the Five Steps in an adult enrichment class might not work in other meeting situations such as at a party, a grocery store, or a library. Different situations might call for different ways of applying the Five Steps. Even though the way the Five Steps are applied might change from one meeting situation to another, however, the purpose of each step remains the same. Let's go over the Five Steps again, but this time we will emphasize the purpose of each step. Once you understand each step you will be better able to customize the Five Steps for any meeting situation.

STEP 1—SEARCH

Purpose

View the men at an event and select the man (or men) you want to meet.

Searching is especially important at big events. At a small house party, you would see all of the men there without making a special effort. At a social event with hundreds of people, searching becomes more important.

When to Search

In situations where you will be seated (lectures, conferences, business meetings), you must select a man and get near him during those times when you aren't fixed in one place. This usually means searching before being seated, during breaks, and after the event. In situations where you are free to move about (health clubs, libraries, shopping malls), when you search is not as critical.

How to Search

One way to search is to sit or stand in one spot and watch men pass by. For example, at a ski resort, stand near a lift line. At a park or shopping mall, sit on a bench and watch men pass by. Sometimes you can search effectively by being mobile. At a ski resort, ski various runs. At a dance, search by walking through the crowd. At a large park, search on your bike.

To help you learn the Five Steps, we will give examples of how to do each step at two different places: a large party and a symphony concert. Here's how to search at these places:

At a large party: Stand by the refreshment table or in some other location where men will pass by, or move around from place to place.

At a concert: Arrive early, wait in the lobby, and watch men coming in. Note any appealing man who is not in the company of a woman. Note where this unaccompanied man sits, so you can search near that section during the intermissions or after the concert. Search the lobby area again during the breaks and after the concert.

STEP 2—GET NEAR

Purpose

Get near enough to start a conversation.

It may seem obvious that you have to get near a man before you can talk to him, but do you do so? How many times have you seen a man you would love to meet, then remained rooted in place daydreaming about him instead of simply moving within speaking distance? This simple, obvious step is necessary before you can make any progress in meeting the man you have selected.

Be alert for opportunities to get near men you'd like to meet. At a busy post office, take a number, find an attractive man, and get near him. You have to wait somewhere; it might as well be by someone you'd like to get to know. If you are in a grocery store and an interesting man is reading the label on a can of green beans, develop a sudden need for a can of green beans.

Here's how to get near at our two sample places:

At a large party: If he's standing, stand near him; if he's sitting, sit near him. If he's in a conversation with a group, join the conversation. If he's at the punch bowl, go get some punch.

At a concert: Before the concert, during intermissions, or after the concert, work your way through the crowd and stand close to him. If he's discussing the concert with a group, stand nearby and show an interest in their conversation. If he's in line at a drinking fountain, get in line behind him.

Meredith did the "get near" step one night and met the man who would become her husband.

Wade and I met at a big singles hangout. He was sitting at the bar and I was across the room at a table with my girlfriends. When I saw Wade looking at me, I met his gaze for a second and then glanced away. We exchanged glances several times, but he didn't come over to my table. I decided to make it easy for him. I got up as if I were headed to the restroom and intentionally walked by him. When I passed in front of Wade, he touched my arm and said, "Hey there, lady! I want to talk to you." After talking for two hours, we left together. I'm not going to tell you what we did, but I never had a relationship take off that fast before. After we got married Wade told me that if I hadn't walked by that night, we wouldn't have met. He said he didn't have the nerve to come over to my table and start a conversation in front of my friends.

Wade didn't have enough nerve to get near Meredith, but when she got near him, he took advantage of the opportunity and spoke to her. Wade, like most men, was afraid to walk up to a table full of women and talk to one of them. When Meredith got away from her friends and put herself close to him, however, he was able to take the initiative to start a conversation.

STEP 3—BREAK THE ICE

Purpose
Get a conversation started.

Say you have gotten near an interesting man in a bookstore, and the two of you are browsing side-by-side. If you wait for him to start a conversation, you may be disappointed. Even if he's aware of your presence and wants to meet you, his fear of rejection could keep him browsing in silence. By simply turning to the man and saying something, you can convert a stranger into an acquaintance, and possibly into much more.

Planned Icebreakers
When you are near an attractive man, the stress of the moment may prevent you from thinking of something to say. You will be less likely to get in this situation if, before you even go out, you plan one or more icebreakers you can use. Here are some examples of icebreakers you could think of ahead of time:

At a large party:
"Hi! How are you doing tonight? My name is Jill."
"How do you know the host?"
"Do you know anyone here?"

At a concert:
"This should be a good concert."

"Are you enjoying the concert?"

"Have you heard this orchestra before?"

Tip: *Write your favorite icebreakers on a card (provided in Appendix B) and carry it with you. Review your icebreakers just before going into a place.*

Spontaneous Icebreakers

After you arrive, be alert for a spontaneous icebreaker that you might prefer to use instead of your planned icebreaker. A spontaneous icebreaker can be a comment on the event, the man's clothes, the weather, or anything else that comes to mind. With a planned icebreaker as a backup and a spontaneous icebreaker when you can think of one, you will not be at a loss for something to say to get a conversation started. Icebreakers do not have to be clever or impressive. If a man is interested in meeting you, almost anything you say will get a conversation started.

STEP 4—CONTINUE THE CONVERSATION

Purpose

Have a relaxed conversation directed toward achieving specific goals.

Monica often has brief chats with men she meets while walking her dog in the park. She complained that these conversations never go anywhere. Here is what she told us:

It happens all the time. I see an interesting man walking toward me. He smiles as he gets close, and we both stop when he asks, "What kind of dog is that?"

"He's a Sheltie."

"He has beautiful markings. What's his name?"

"Laddie."

"Cute name."

Soon there is a brief pause, which makes standing there a

little awkward. Then the man will say something like, "Well, have a nice day."

"You, too."

I've been walking Laddie in the park for two years and I've never had a date with a man I met there.

Monica's experience points out a common problem that can occur when you meet a man in a "passing by" situation such as in a park or shopping mall. When you are face-to-face with an attractive man, your emotions can make it difficult to keep the conversation going. If he is having the same problem, an awkward silence can develop that can end the conversation. Avoid this by having specific conversation goals. Direct the conversation to achieve these goals.

The following four conversation goals will give you valuable information about the man and help you keep the conversation flowing as you transform a casual conversation into something more meaningful.

Conversation Goal No. 1—Get Insurance

Insurance is information that "insures" you can contact a man at a later time in case neither of you gets a chance to close. It's a way to reach someone again when a conversation gets cut short.

Sometimes a man's first name and his place of work are all you need to know. For example, if his name is Brian and he works at Westside Real Estate, you will probably be able to reach him by calling Westside Real Estate and saying, "Could I please speak to Brian?" If he works for a large company, however, his first name and the name of his company might not be enough. For example, if all you know is that his name is Brian and he works for Proctor and Gamble, you are out of luck. In this case you need to ask him what department he works in and what he does there. For example, if he says he's a commercial artist and works in the Package Design Department at Proctor and Gamble, you will probably have success reaching him by calling Proctor and Gamble and saying, "I'd like to speak to Brian in Package Design." If the person who answers the phone in Package Design says, "I'm sorry, we have two Brians. What's his last name?" you can describe your Brian and say he's a commercial artist. Most people are willing to be helpful in these situations.

If the man doesn't have a fixed place of employment, you might not be able to get insurance simply by asking questions about his work. When this happens you have to be creative. For example, if he says, "I'm a free-lance photographer. Weddings are my specialty," you still don't have the information you need to be able to reach him later. You could say, however, "I have a friend who is getting married. Could I give her your card?"

It is also helpful to get a man's first and last name. Once you have his full name it will be easy to reach him when he is at work, or you can look him up in the phone book and call him at home. If you don't mind giving out your last name, introduce yourself by your full name, and the man will probably do the same. "Hi! I'm Alice" will usually get the response, "I'm Ted." "Hi! I'm Alice Barnet" will usually be answered by, "I'm Ted Hughes."

Tip: If you introduce yourself by your first and last name and the man seems hesitant about giving out his last name, this is your first clue that he might be married or living with someone. His hesitancy might mean he doesn't want you looking up his home number and embarrassing him with a call at home.

In addition to times when neither of you has a chance to arrange a date, insurance is also useful in situations where setting a date may seem inappropriate or awkward. Clara found herself in just such a situation one night. Here is what she told us:

One evening I stopped in a jazz bar with Eric, a friend of mine from work. Eric and I aren't romantically involved; we both just wanted to listen to some jazz. In the bar, this dreamboat of a man sat next to me and we started talking. After a while I could tell he was interested in me. I could also tell he thought Eric was my boyfriend. I suppose I could have explained the situation, but I didn't think of it at the time. After about an hour he left, with a "See you later." The next day, I realized I knew his first name and the company he worked for, so I found his company in the phone book and called. I got transferred three times before finally reaching him. He accepted my invitation to meet for lunch, and we have been seeing each other ever since.

You probably don't run into these dreamboat men very often, so make it a habit to always get insurance. Once you have insurance, you have the choice of using it or not.

Conversation Goal No. 2—Qualify Him

If people were made in factories and you could order a love partner manufactured to your exact specifications, you would probably spend a great deal of time thinking about the type of man you really want. But since you can't order exactly what you want, you may not have given much thought to the characteristics you desire in a partner. You may just be hoping to meet "someone." The type of man you get involved with doesn't have to be left entirely to chance, however, you do have some control over this matter.

Decide what you are looking for, and then, during your initial conversation with a man, ask questions to see if he meets your requirements. When you ask these questions, you are "qualifying" him as a potential partner. You might ask questions to find out such things as:

Is he married?

Does he have children?

Where does he live?

What does he do for a living?

What are his favorite hobbies and activities?

These or other issues may be important to you. To get the information you need, ask your questions in a way that doesn't make him feel as if he's being interrogated. Ask one question, and then talk about that subject for a few minutes before going on to your next question. He will probably be flattered that you're showing an interest in him, and relieved that the conversation is going so well.

Connie is a student of ours who just turned forty. She has been married twice and doesn't plan on having children. When asked what she wants in a man, she said, "I don't need a man to support me. What I'm looking for is a man who will share my life. Common interests, intimacy, and companionship are of high value to me." Connie used a form to list her requirements that we included in our class handout.

A few weeks after taking our class, Connie told us how she was using her requirements to qualify the men she meets.

> I used to spend a lot of time with a man and then find out he's not suitable for me. That was hard on my emotions and a waste of my time—time I could have spent finding a suitable man. I now know what type of man I want, and when I first meet a man, I make a conscious effort to find out if he has the characteristics I'm looking for. In addition to asking all the standard questions about where he lives and what he does for a living, I open myself up and reveal something personal about myself, then I note what he says in response and how he says it.
>
> Let me give you an example. Cooking a great variety of different recipes and exploring ethnic restaurants are among my main interests in life. It's a high priority for me to find a man who will share these interests. It's not important that a man enjoy cooking, even though that would be nice, but it is important that he enjoy my cooking and share my interest in trying a variety of cuisines. To find out if a man shares these interests, I tell him about how much these things mean to me, and then I analyze his response.

Here are actual responses Connie received from different men (and her reactions):

CONNIE: "I really love to cook. I have a cookbook collection you wouldn't believe, probably forty books on all kinds of

The Type of Man I Want to Meet

Category	Connie's Requirements
Age	35–45 would be nice.
Marital History	Divorced or never married. It doesn't matter.
Children	Okay for him to have kids.
Religion	Humanist type is best (a devoutly religious man won't do).
Geographic	Anywhere in the metropolitan area.
Smoking	Nonsmoker a must.
Drinking	No evidence of alcohol abuse. Non- or light drinkers get extra points.
Drug Use	No drug use.
Education	The more the better.
Occupation	White collar (I'm more in tune with them.)
Financial Status	Wealth is not an issue. Good money management is what counts.
Character	He should be honest, thoughtful, and affectionate, have an inquisitive nature, and be open to new experiences.
Type of Relationship	He should want a monogamous relationship and be open to marriage. This is critical.
Interests	It's important that he enjoy a wide variety of cuisines, enjoy foreign and domestic travel, and love reading.

cuisines. I have recipes from all over the world. It's so much fun to find a new recipe and try it out."

MAN NO. 1: "Oh." (*Definitely a bad sign—he can't even think of a response.*)

MAN NO. 2: "I like to fish." (*Two bad signs: he's not interested in exploring new foods, and he's not interested in talking about my interests.*)

MAN NO. 3: (during a phone conversation in response to my personal ad): "Are you fat?" (*This is the worst. He's not interested in what I have to say, and he's shallow and rude.*)

MAN NO. 4: "I'm not a great cook, but I'm definitely a gourmet eater." (*Good sign. He'll probably eat any exotic dish I cook.*)

MAN NO. 5: "Oh, I love to cook too. What's your specialty?" (*A great sign. This guy has possibilities.*)

Connie also felt it was important that a man be open-minded and willing to try different activities. "I don't want to spend ten years with a man waiting for him to open up to life's experiences," she said. "I tried that before, and it didn't work. I don't have ten years to waste this time. To find out if a man is open to new experiences, I describe some of my activities and then analyze his responses." Here are some of the responses Connie got (and her reactions to them).

CONNIE: "Boy, have I been busy the past few weeks. The past two Saturdays I went on hikes with the Mountain Club. Last week I attended a book discussion group and took in a slide show at the Museum of Natural History. Two weeks ago I took a class on forensic anthropology—it was great. I'm also taking country dance lessons."

MAN NO. 1: "Just think what you could accomplish if you weren't doing all that stuff." (*A bad sign. I felt put down.*)

MAN NO. 2: "How did you find out about all those activities?" (*A good sign. He may be interested in such an active life.*)

MAN NO. 3: "Wow! You do a lot of interesting things, especially that book discussion group. Could I come along sometime?" (*A very good sign. He seems interested in books and interested in me.*)

Connie thought that filling out her requirements list helped her focus on what kind of man she really wanted. Her method of qualifying a man by bringing up a subject and watching his reaction is subtle. She now does this automatically whenever she meets a man and feels certain that men don't know what she is doing. The last time we heard from Connie she was dating a college professor who likes to cook.

Before you qualify a man, you need to know what you are looking for. A blank "requirements" form, like the one Connie filled out, is available in Appendix A to help you determine the characteristics of the man you want.

Conversation Goal No. 3—Drop Hints

This goal is not needed if you know you are going to close. If you're not sure that you have the nerve to close or if you would prefer that the man ask you out, however, dropping the right hints will make it more likely he will ask you out.

Hint That You Like Him

A man who is afraid of rejection will look for clear signs that you are interested in him. A hint can show your interest:

At a large party: "You have a great sense of humor. I really enjoy listening to your stories."

At a concert: (as you gently touch his arm): "I wish we could talk longer. I'd like to hear more about your trip to Africa."

Hint About Activities You Enjoy

A man may be more likely to ask you out if he has an idea for a date that he knows you will enjoy. Here's how to hint about activities you enjoy:

At a large party: "I just read a review of a movie I'd like to see."

At a concert: "Next week the Calgary Choir will be appearing with the symphony. That would be a great performance to see."

Conversation Goal No. 4—Extend Your Time Together

In some meeting situations you might want to get to know a man better before suggesting a future date, but it is inconvenient to talk where you are. When this happens, try to find a way to extend your time together. For example, if you meet a man in a grocery store, you might feel awkward standing in the aisle having a long conversation. In this case you could suggest meeting at a nearby coffee shop after you finish shopping. Extending your time together is an excellent way to make a gradual and smooth transition from a casual encounter to something more significant. Here are some other examples of ways to extend your time together:

At a large party: "Would you like to go out on the patio where it's quiet?"

At a concert: "Would you like to meet for a drink after the concert?"

When you are talking with a man you have just met, you can't be sure how long the conversation will last. You may have only a few minutes to bring this special person into your life. Make the most of this initial conversation by striving to achieve the four conversation goals.

Here's what Ann had to say about how these conversation goals helped her:

I used to dread going to singles events. The thing I hated most was all the aimless small talk. I had a vague feeling that I should be accomplishing something when I talked to men, but I didn't know what it was. Was I supposed to flatter the man, impress him, entertain him, or what? Knowing the four conversation goals got me away from the small talk and gave the conversations meaning.

STEP 5—CLOSE

Purpose
Arrange to see him again.

For simplicity, we call the process of arranging future contact "closing." You might think that you can leave the closing up to the man, assuming that he will ask you out if he is interested in you. There are two big problems with this, however:

♦ He may be interested in you, but his fear of rejection keeps him from asking you out.

♦ He may not yet know if he's interested.

If he is interested in you and you close, he will probably accept and be thrilled that you asked. If he hasn't made up his mind and you close, you have helped him make a decision. It is now easier for him to accept your offer than to say no. There are two effective ways for a woman to close:

Close No. 1—Suggest an Activity and Give Him Your Number

There's little chance of immediate rejection when you suggest an activity and give a man your number. Even if he's not interested, he will usually smile and thank you. If he is interested, there's an excellent chance he will call. Here's how this technique could be used:

At a large party: "If you would like to get together sometime, give me a call. Here's my work number. It's OK to call me there."

At a concert: "If you decide you would like to see the Calgary Choir when they come to town, maybe we could go together. I'll write down my number."

Tip: *You may want to limit the information you give a man. You don't have to give him your full name, and you don't have to tell him where you live. You can just give him your first name and your work or home number, whichever you prefer.*

Close No. 2—Ask for a Date

When you ask a man for a date, you risk immediate rejection. You also immediately find out if he's interested, however, and you won't have to sit around wondering if he's going to call. Here are some ways to ask for a date:

At a large party: "Would you like to meet at the Willow Tavern on Thursday for a drink after work?"

At a concert: "Would you like to see the Calgary Choir with me next week?"

Directly asking for a date might result either in rejection or in a date with a very suitable man. Forget the myth about men not liking aggressive women. Being asked for a date is a nice compliment.

In our class, after we have explained the Five Steps and recommended that women take the initiative in the meeting process, we get reactions such as:

"I don't want to come on strong and look like a pushy, obnoxious woman."

"I could do the first four steps, but I'm not going to go for the kill."

And a woman who had taken our class earlier said,

"When I told my mother about the Five Steps she said, 'Don't you dare ask a man out.'"

Okay, so taking the initiative is not what your mother said to do, but it is what we say to do. We recommend it because we know that it's effective—we know it works. Here is what Samantha said about taking the initiative and using the Five Steps:

> At first taking the initiative was scary; now it's second nature. And men don't have a clue that I'm using the Five Steps. They only know that somehow they ended up talking to me, and maybe ended up with my number or a date. Most of the time they are just happy to have met someone. For me it's a great relief to know what to do when I see a man I want to meet. I can't imagine sitting there like a bump on a log waiting for a man to approach me. That's demeaning.

One time we had an occasion to see Samantha in action, and she was not pushy or obnoxious. Quite the opposite—she took the initiative in a subtle way that made the conversation pleasant and relaxed.

Many women are also concerned that someone nearby will know that they are actively trying to meet a man. We have heard many comments such as:

> "What would people think if they saw me doing that?"

> "They will know what I'm doing."

> "I might do the Five Steps if no one knew what I was doing."

We know this concern is real and powerful because we have heard these comments so often. It's a myth, however, that "they will see me and know what I am doing." In a singles place, "they," the other people present, are too busy dealing with their own meeting and rejection concerns to care about what you are doing. Besides, there is no way for another person to tell that the Five Steps are being used. The actions related to executing each of the Five Steps are common in social settings. Only you will know that you are putting these actions together for a specific goal.

Your fear of taking the initiative in the meeting process is understandable. Most men face this fear and know how strong it is. Many of our students, however, women as well as men, know this fear is something one can gradually overcome. Although the fear may never completely go away, it can often be reduced to a point where it is no longer so immobilizing that it prevents you from taking the initiative.

First Date Safety

When arranging a first date with a man they don't know well, some women are obviously concerned about their safety, while others hardly give it a thought. For example, Jill, a graduate student, would only agree to a one-on-one date with a man after several "nonromantic" group social interactions with him. Jill said she wanted to know a man pretty well before going out on the first date. At the other end of the safety spectrum was a woman Ken met on a bike path.

One summer evening as I was riding my bike through a forest preserve, I saw a woman riding ahead of me. I wasn't sure if I should approach her because the sun had gone down. I sometimes startle women when I ride up beside them in broad daylight. With it getting dark, I was afraid I would scare this woman to death. I decided to approach her anyway, and if she wasn't obviously open to my company, I would quickly ride on.

"Nice night," I said as I rode up beside her. "It's beautiful out," she said with a big smile. Encouraged by her response, I rode beside her and continued talking. After about ten minutes of conversation with lots of positive feedback, I offered a "mini-date." I said, "I'm going to take the path around the lake. Want to join me?" "Sure," she said, and off we went. Twenty minutes later we were riding through the woods on a dark and deserted bike path. I was amazed that she was so trusting.

The graduate student had to have several group social interactions with a man before agreeing to a date, while the woman on the bike path trusted a man from the first hello. If you are somewhere between these extremes, here are some suggestions to help you make a first date safer without turning the guy off.

A First Date Safety Plan

1. Get Identifying Information About Him, and Verify It

When you introduce yourself to a man, get his first and last name. During your initial conversation, weave in questions about where he works, what he does there, and how long he has been with that company. You can also learn what part of town he lives in and what organizations he belongs to. Later, when a date is being arranged, request both his home and work phone numbers (tell him you want to be able to reach him in case something comes up and you need to change the date).

Once you have this information, you can check as much of it as you want. You can call the personnel department of his company and verify his employment. Many personnel departments will also give out an employee's position and years of employment. A phone call will also verify his membership in an organization. If he is in the phone book, see if the address and phone number match what he gave you. Call him at home or at work to confirm the specifics of the date. If any of the information he gave you turns out to be false, it's obviously reason for concern.

Some women go to great lengths to check out a man. For example, Sandy said, "Before I go out with a man, I always call the Department of Motor Vehicles and check on his driving record. I avoid any man who has been convicted of drunk driving or reckless driving, or whose driver's license has been revoked."

2. Limit His Ability to Contact You

If you date a man for a while, he will eventually know your full name, home phone, home address, work phone, and where you work. He doesn't need this information for the first date, however, or even for the first several dates if you want it that way. Without such information, he has less ability to give you unwanted attention. Depending on your comfort level, you can give him as much or as little information as you want. Stay in control of the situation; you decide when he gets additional information.

To minimize the information you give a man, arrange to meet him somewhere for the first date. Since he isn't going to pick you up, he doesn't need to know your address. The only information you have to give him is your first name.

An even more cautious approach is to delay a decision on when and where the first date will be. When he asks you out, say, "I would like to go out with you. Give me your number and I'll call you later in the week when I know my schedule." You will then have time to verify information about him and to talk to him on the phone a time or two before arranging a date.

3. Make the Activity on Your First Date Safe

Dorothy grew up in a small town in Maine and spent her high school years dating the townies. After graduation, she moved to California and got an apartment in Hollywood. She was there only a couple of weeks before she had some interesting stories to tell:

> Hollywood was sure a far cry from Bar Harbor. In Hollywood I saw men picking up men on the streets and heading into fleabag hotels. I saw hypodermic syringes under the sewer grates, and when I was just walking down the street one night, a crazy man waved a gun in my face.
>
> Despite this quick education, my trusting small-town habits died hard. One night I met a man in a jazz bar and accepted a date to go shooting in the national forest the next day. As we drove to the forest, I started having serious misgivings about

what I was doing. When the misgivings escalated to panic, I told him I was having a migraine attack and would have to go home immediately. He argued with me, obviously not wanting to give up his trip to the woods with this naive small-town girl. He refused to turn around until I flew into a rage.

There are few dates you could make that would show worse judgment than Dorothy's. After you have made a date to be alone in the woods with a man with a gun whom you met in a bar in a bad part of town, you have nowhere to go but up. Obviously, Dorothy did not arrange a safe first-date activity. To make your first-date activity safer:

♦ Meet the man there so you won't have to get in his car.
♦ Meet him during daylight hours.
♦ Meet him in a busy public place.

For peace of mind more than safety, you might also want to arrange a short first date that has a fixed end time. A short date will be a relief if things don't go well, and with a fixed end time you won't have to think up an excuse for ending the date.

Tip: *Meeting a man for lunch makes a good first date. Lunch is a daytime activity that can be in a public place with a fixed end time. Meeting a man for drinks after work is also a good first date. If things don't go well, you can excuse yourself after a brief stay. On the other hand, if you are enjoying his company, you can suggest that the two of you have dinner together.*

There is an additional precaution you can take. Tell a friend about your upcoming date and give her all the information you have about the man. Then tell the man that a friend (unnamed) knows that you are on a date with him and has this information. You might think that he will be indignant at your lack of trust. He probably will react the way John did, however:

On the first date I had with Vi, we were driving to a movie when she looked at me and said, "I told my friend all about you, and I told her we were going out tonight." I didn't get the drift of what Vi was telling me until she added, "I wanted her to have this information in case something happened to me. This is just something I do before I go out with a man I don't know very well. I hope you understand."

That was the first time a woman had ever said anything like that to me. It had never occurred to me that a woman might actually be afraid to go out with me. I certainly wasn't upset with her. I thought it was a pretty clever way for her to make sure she got home safe and sound.

Here are examples of conversations you might have as you implement our safety suggestions:

He asks: "Would you like to go out sometime?"
You reply: "Yes, let's meet for lunch. Give me your phone number and I'll call you early next week after I check my Day-Timer."

(You took charge, got his number, and gave yourself some time to verify information. He has no information about you except possibly your first name.)

He asks: "Maybe we could get together for dinner next week. If you give me your number, I'll call you."
You reply: "Next week is a busy week for me. Would it be okay if we met for drinks after work instead? Say around six on Tuesday at Bender's Pub? Just in case something comes up, could I have your number?"

(You have changed a long, possibly formal dinner date into a short, informal date in which you can control the time you leave. You are meeting him there, so he won't have to pick you up.)

He asks: "Want to go dancing tomorrow night?
You reply: "Dancing sounds great. Let's meet at Rico Reds at eight-thirty. And I'd better get your number, just in case I get delayed."

(You got his phone number and arranged to meet him there.)

He asks: "By the way, Mary, I don't believe you gave me your last name."
You reply: "I'd feel more comfortable telling you that after I know you better. I hope you understand."

(You have limited his ability to reach you by not giving your last name.)

He says: (after a meeting has been arranged): "I'll meet you there. In case an emergency comes up, I'd better get your number."
You say: "For now, I'd rather just take your number. If you don't show up, I'll call you and we'll schedule the date for another time."

(You got his number and avoided giving out yours.)

There are few things you do in life that are 100 percent safe, but with some thought and preparation, most activities, including going on a first date, can be made safer. Take control of the situation. Make a safer first date by getting information about the man, verifying it, and limiting his ability to contact you.

5

How to Work As a Team

When most women go out "looking" with a friend, they have a tendency to socialize with their friend instead of concentrating on the meeting process. Although this can be fun, it's not an effective way to meet someone. There are three ways to be more effective:

1. Go out alone.
2. Go with a friend, but split up when you get there.
3. Go with a friend and apply the Five Steps as a team.

Working as a team can be just as effective as working alone— sometimes even more so. Here is a true-life example of two people working as a team: Barry and Cindy knew each other from work. Barry was dating someone; Cindy was single and looking. One day Cindy learned about a wine-tasting party being held after work at a nearby hotel. She arranged to have Barry meet her there because she wanted to see what the party was like, but was afraid to be there alone. When Barry arrived at the party he found Cindy standing against the wall holding a glass of wine, not talking to anyone. Here's what happened next:

BARRY: "Hi, Cindy. You don't look like you're having much fun."

CINDY: "Nobody's come over to talk to me, and I don't know how to get a conversation going with a man whom I don't know. I'm really nervous. I feel so obvious standing here alone."

BARRY: "Well, let's see if I can help you. Do you see anyone you'd like to meet?"

CINDY (*looking around the room*): "I'd like to meet that man standing over there."

BARRY: "Come with me. Let's see what we can do."

The man Cindy picked out—we'll call him the "selected" man— was in a conversation with a woman and another man. Because the event was crowded, Barry, with Cindy in tow, was able to move close to the selected man without attracting attention.

CINDY (*whispering in Barry's ear*): "What are you going to say?"

BARRY (*whispering*): "I'm going to talk about his sport coat. No, I'm going to talk about his tie—it's a flowered tie just like mine. Now, when I get this going, don't drop the ball. You have to jump in quick."

CINDY (*still whispering*): "Okay, but that woman—what about her?"

BARRY: "Don't worry about her. You'll blow her away. You look great."

The selected man continued talking with the other two people. After a few minutes there was a pause in their conversation. Barry, taking advantage of this pause, turned to the selected man and looked at his tie.

BARRY: "I see you like wild ties, too."

SELECTED MAN (*looking down at his tie*): "You know, a woman at work helps me pick out my clothes. I don't really know the styles, and I don't think I have very good taste."

CINDY (*jumping right in*): "A woman from work helps you pick out your clothes? That's interesting. Where do you work?"

Cindy and the man discovered that they both worked for the state; she as a social worker and he as a highway engineer. Working for the state gave them something to talk about. After a few minutes, the other woman and man sensed that they had been cut out of the conversation, so they started a conversation between themselves. Barry stayed around just long enough to be of help one more time. He introduced himself to the selected man (Steve), and then introduced Steve to Cindy. Barry then said he had spotted a friend he hadn't seen in a long time and departed, leaving Steve and Cindy alone. (Note that Cindy started addressing her conversation goals with her opening comment, "A woman from work helps you pick out your clothes? That's interesting. Where do you work?" Steve's answer gave her a start on getting insurance, as well as some qualifying information.)

At work the next day Cindy told Barry, "Steve asked me out to dinner. We're going out tomorrow night. You sure made that easy for me. I'll bet I could help you meet any woman the same way you helped me meet Steve. That teamwork is great."

Working as a team *is* great because the Five Steps can be divided between two people in a way that makes the meeting process easier. In a team, one person is helping a friend meet someone. We call the helper the *facilitator*. Your facilitator can be any male or female friend of yours. We call the person trying to meet someone the *aspirant*. In the story above, Barry was the facilitator and Cindy was the aspirant. Here's how the facilitator and aspirant apply the Five Steps as a team.

Step 1—Search (Performed by Aspirant)

The aspirant chooses someone desirable to meet and points that person out to the facilitator. In the above example, Cindy looked around, saw a man she wanted to meet, and pointed him out to Barry.

Step 2—Get Near (Performed by Facilitator)

The facilitator takes the initiative to get near the selected person. In our example, Barry led Cindy over to where they could stand close to the selected man. Barry could do this without hesitation because he had nothing riding on the outcome of the venture.

Step 3—Break the Ice (Performed by Facilitator)

The facilitator says something to the selected person to get a conversation started, and then the aspirant joins the conversation. With little at stake, it's fairly easy for the facilitator to start a conversation. In the example, Barry broke the ice with the selected man by noting that they both were wearing flowered ties.

Step 4—Continue the Conversation (Aspirant Takes Over)

Now it is up to the aspirant to engage the selected person in a conversation and address the conversation goals of getting insurance, qualifying, and dropping hints, extending their time together.

If the aspirant wants to be left alone with the selected person to carry on the conversation and possibly close, the facilitator should help set up this one-on-one situation. If the selected person was alone before being approached by the team, once the aspirant is in the conversation the facilitator can simply make an excuse and leave. If the selected person was with others before being approached, the facilitator can attempt to draw the others into a separate conversation, leaving the aspirant and selected person to themselves. Before approaching the selected person, the aspirant and facilitator should discuss what the facilitator will do once the conversation has started.

In the above story, even though Steve (the selected man) was initially in a conversation with two others, Barry was able to leave because the two others had started a separate conversation between themselves. Since the desired isolation of Cindy with Steve had already been achieved, Barry's help was no longer needed.

Tip: *If you want the selected man to ask you out, your facilitator should leave soon after the conversation has started, because most men prefer to ask for a date in a one-on-one situation. Besides, if your facilitator is a woman, the selected man may not know which of you is interested in him, or worse, he may get interested in the facilitator instead of you. If you are with a male facilitator, the selected man might think the two of you are involved. To clear up any confusion and give the guy a chance to ask you out without an audience, the facilitator should leave.*

Step 5—Close (Performed by Aspirant)

At this point the aspirant is typically alone with the selected person. The close is performed as in any other meeting situation. In our story, Cindy didn't have to close because the selected man, Steve, asked her out to dinner.

Working as a team is effective because the facilitator, with nothing riding on the outcome, has no fear of rejection and can therefore more easily come up with unique, clever, and even bold ways to get near and break the ice, thus sparing the aspirant these sometimes difficult steps. Your facilitator can be involved with someone else (as Barry was in the example) or looking. If both you and your friend are looking, take turns being the facilitator.

The next time you go out "looking" with a friend, don't just stand there in idle conversation with your companion friend while you wait to get lucky. Create your own luck by working as a team. It's easy, sometimes even fun, and definitely effective.

6

Where to Go

*I*n our classes, after we have just mentioned a dozen or so places where singles can meet, a student will often say, "I have tried all those places. Tell us some more places to go." What the student really means is, "I have tried the places you suggested, was uncomfortable in all of them, and didn't meet anybody. Tell me about an 'ideal' place where I will feel at ease and where it will be easy to meet and get a date with an attractive, quality person." No wonder our students want to hear about more places to go. None of the places we mention come close to this ideal place (in reality, it is unlikely that such a place even exists).

Rather than search for this elusive ideal place, you should focus on places in the real world. Each place will have its advantages and disadvantages—none will be perfect. You might feel more comfortable in some places than in others. Some will have more desirable men than others. A combination of factors is what makes one place better than another for any given woman, no one place is best for everyone. One woman might be sold on meeting men at a health club, another loves the dance places. One swears that adult enrichment classes are best, another feels that church is best. Your job is to find the places that are good for you. It is unlikely that just one place will meet all of your needs. Many women go to a variety of places.

To help choose which places to try, ask the following questions:

♦ Is the place for singles or nonsingles?
♦ Will the ratio of men to women be favorable?
♦ Will compatible men be there?
♦ Will quality men be there?
♦ Will the men be the right age?
♦ Will the social setting be good for meeting a man?

Note
We sometimes use the term "place" in a generalized sense to mean any location, event, class, or organization where there are men.

IS THE PLACE FOR SINGLES OR NONSINGLES?

At a "singles" place, the majority of those present will be single men and women hoping to meet the opposite sex. Singles mixers, singles bars, singles clubs, and singles dances are definitely in this category. Sometimes events such as street fairs, wine-tasting parties, and after-work jazz concerts also catch on as places for singles to mix and mingle.

Most people at a "nonsingles" place will be there for reasons other than to try to meet the opposite sex. Examples of nonsingles places are museums, parks, churches, bike paths, and gatherings of organizations that don't cater to singles.

Some places don't fit neatly into either the singles or nonsingles category. For example, a folk dance club may have some members who are married or involved with someone and many other members who are single and attend folk dances hoping to meeting someone.

Advantages of Singles Places
Singles places offer several advantages over nonsingles places. The majority of the men at a singles place are available and interested in meeting a woman. You are more likely to be approached by a man in a singles place because men are usually there for one reason—to meet a woman. Therefore, you may be successful using just the Passive Technique and waiting to be approached.

If you choose to use the Active Technique (which we do recommend), you may feel more confident at a singles place because you know that the men there are probably available and interested in meeting a woman. If you start a conversation with a man, you won't have to be concerned that his wife or girlfriend will show up and wonder what you are doing. You can't be sure of this in a nonsingles place. For instance, if you start a conversation with a man in a shopping mall, you might get a surprise when his wife returns. For most women, trying to meet a man at a singles place seems less threatening than in a nonsingles place. At a singles place everyone knows why everyone else is there, and the layout of the place often encourages socializing.

Advantages of Nonsingles Places

Singles places can sometimes have a "meat-market" atmosphere where the men look you over and compare you to all the other women. There is no meat-market atmosphere at a nonsingles place. Men who go to singles places regularly are exposed to many dating opportunities. This makes some of them very selective. A man in a nonsingles place might not be exposed to many opportunities to meet women, and as a result, he might be especially receptive if you start a conversation with him.

Carol, a friend of ours who is an avid reader of self-help books, thinks the advantages of nonsingles places go unnoticed:

In all the books for singles that I have read, the advantages of meeting in nonsingles places were never mentioned. All they talk about is going to singles functions.

Personally, I don't like the feeling of singles functions, and I find that nonsingles places offer several advantages over singles places. I meet higher quality men at nonsingles places (men who would probably reject me in a singles environment), and I meet men whom I wouldn't meet anywhere else because they don't go to singles functions. I also feel that meeting a man in a nonsingles place is more romantic. For instance, striking up a conversation with a man in an outdoor café seems more romantic to me than talking to a man in a singles discussion group.

I also have more luck in nonsingles places. For example, last week I went to a travel lecture. The speaker was a journalist who recently emigrated from Russia. After the lecture, I introduced myself and told him how much I enjoyed his lecture. He told me that he was attempting to organize another lecture series. I know a man who I thought could help him, so I gave him my contact's number, along with my number, in case he needed a recommendation. Yesterday he called, and after we talked for an hour, he asked me out. I'm really excited. He is a hunk.

WILL THE RATIO OF MEN TO WOMEN BE FAVORABLE?

A favorable ratio of men to women is sometimes important and sometimes not. If you use the Passive Technique and wait for a man to approach you, a favorable ratio is bound to help. If you use the Active Technique and approach the man of your choice, however, the men-to-women ratio is less important. Judy, a former student of ours, told us that she doesn't give the ratio a second thought:

Last Sunday I went to a picnic sponsored by a singles organization. As usual for events sponsored by this group, women outnumbered men three to one, but that no longer bothers me. I moved around socializing, and talked to every man there. I didn't feel attracted to any of them, and I was about to leave for an appointment with my realtor when I saw a new arrival at the buffet table. I decided it was time to get more salad.

As I was putting a little salad on my plate, I said to him, "You're lucky there's still some food left." He smiled and we started talking. I knew I liked him and I thought he liked me. But I couldn't wait around to see if he would ask me out because I was pressed for time. So after a couple of minutes, I handed him my business card and said, "I have to go now to meet my realtor. Give me a call so we can talk later." He said he would call me next week, after he got back from vacation.

If you use the Passive Technique and wait to be approached, a picnic with three times as many women as men may not be very productive. With the Active Technique, the ratio is of little importance.

WILL COMPATIBLE MEN BE THERE?

Many compatibility characteristics have obvious connections with places to go. If you want to meet a man of a certain religion, attend church and church-related activities. If you enjoy gardening and would like to meet a man with a similar interest, try a gardening club and lectures on gardening. Like to sail? Try a sailing club. Given your requirements, and some thought, you can often find a surprising number of places where compatible men might be.

Connie, a student of ours, feels she would be most compatible with an educated, intelligent man who enjoys reading, cooking, and exploring ethnic restaurants. She had this to say about how she intends to meet such a man:

> I felt real clever when I realized that the cookbook section of a library or bookstore was one place I could meet a man who likes books and who also enjoys cooking. Adult enrichment classes on cooking are also a possibility.
>
> I will avoid the singles bars. I don't think I would have a good chance of meeting a compatible man there. I think men in singles bars are more likely to smoke, drink, and use drugs. And besides, I hate being in those places because of the smoke. A lot of my friends tell me I should try their church, but I'm not going to do it. I don't think it would work out with a religious man.

Connie has given some thought to where to find a compatible man, and she has a couple of places to start looking. Connie ruled out singles bars and churches as places to meet men for what she felt were good reasons. We suggest, however, that you not be too quick to rule out a place just because it doesn't specifically attract your type of man. Any place with a large number of men is likely to have a least a few who would be compatible with you.

Will Quality Men Be There?

What do women mean when they say they want to meet a "quality" man? Although quality is commonly associated with integrity, education, and profession, each woman's definition would probably be different. Because there are so many different interpretations of what a quality man is, it is difficult to relate "quality" to a certain place where you could meet a man. Even if we assume, for the sake of argument, that a quality man is an educated professional man of high integrity, we would still be hard pressed to say at which places you are most likely to find such a man. From our experience, he could show up at a church social or a lecture, and also at a singles mixer or the local honky-tonk.

Sometimes we see women putting too much emphasis on the quality issue. For example, here is what Audrey told us about her plan for meeting a quality man:

> I'm thirty now and I think it's time to get serious about settling down and starting a family. I've been thinking of places I could go to meet a quality man, and I have an idea. I like to ski, and I would like to meet a man who skis. A local ski resort has a program where people volunteer to teach disabled kids to ski. For every day that you volunteer, you get a free lift ticket. I'm going to volunteer. I figure that if I meet a man who is a volunteer at such an activity, we would have a shared interest in skiing, and he would be a quality person.

Audrey's plan has some flaws. When she told us about her plan, ski season was still four months away, and she had no other strategy for meeting a man. It is unreasonable for her to pin all her hopes for meeting a quality man on one activity that is so far in the future. Besides, when ski season does start she will probably have a very limited number of male volunteers to choose from. The chance that Audrey will find a quality man who is unattached, whom she is attracted to, and who is attracted to her seems too small to put much hope in. It is fine for Audrey to plan on becoming a volunteer at the ski resort, but in the meantime she should put her efforts into exploring other avenues for meeting her quality man.

WILL THE MEN BE THE RIGHT AGE?

Obviously a good place to go is one where most of the men are the right age for you. This doesn't mean, however, that you should only go to places which cater to men in your desired age range. Most singles and nonsingles places attract a wide range of ages. Since you are only looking for one man, you will have a chance of finding him at a place where the men are of many different ages.

WILL THE SOCIAL SETTING BE GOOD FOR MEETING A MAN?

When selecting places to go, consider how easy it will be to mix and mingle there, to start and carry on conversations. That is, how easy will it be for you to meet a man there? At some places it will be relatively easy, at others it will be more difficult. "Sit down" places, such as lectures, films, and concerts, are difficult places to meet a man because mingling times are limited to before the event, during breaks, and after the event. "Stand and browse" places, such as art galleries, museums, and street fairs, offer a better setting for meeting a man because it is possible to move about, get near, and say something to almost any man there. Places with "participation" activities, such as local tours, cooking classes, and dance lessons, sometimes offer the best situations for meeting a man because the nature of the activity causes people to interact with one another. You dance with men in a dance class, you cook with men in a cooking class, and you talk with men on a tour.

FINDING PLACES TO GO

There is no one answer to where you should go. The above advice will help you choose places that are good for you. To give you some ideas on different places where you can go to meet a man, we have a form in Appendix A that you can fill out. This form is called "Where

I Will Go." In Chapter 3 ("The Five Steps") we showed "The Type of Man I Want to Meet" form that Connie (our student who wanted to meet an intellectual man who liked to read, travel, and try various ethnic cuisines) filled out. To help you fill out the blank "Where I Will Go" form in Appendix A, see how Connie completed it (opposite).

The "Where I Will Go" form may give you general ideas about the types of places you want to try. Even though you may know that you want to try certain places, however, how do you find the "where and when" details for specific places near where you live? Say you want to take dance lessons or join a singles hiking club. How do you find out who gives dance lessons or which singles hiking clubs are in your area? We recommend the following four sources of information: entertainment weeklies, daily newspapers, adult enrichment class catalogs, and the yellow pages.

Entertainment Weeklies
These free, singles-oriented newspapers can be found in most metropolitan areas. They often have a calendar showing events and activities for each day of the coming week, plus listings of special events. We recently looked through the most popular entertainment weekly in Denver and found lectures and workshops sponsored by museums, churches, singles clubs, and universities. There were also many concerts, plays, films, and classes listed, as well as museums, galleries, entertainment spots, and singles dances. Entertainment weeklies are the first place many singles look when choosing where to go.

Daily Papers
Daily papers often have an entertainment or "weekend" section in one edition. The activities listed, although similar to those in the entertainment weeklies, are more for the general public and less oriented towards singles. Call the daily papers in your area to see which edition has an entertainment section (usually it is the Friday paper).

Adult Enrichment Class Catalogs
Adult enrichment classes are taken for fun or enlightenment, not for grades or a degree. They are a great way to fill up your calendar

Where I Will Go

(Use Your Requirements as a Guide)
(Y = Yes, N = No, M = Maybe)

Places, Activities, & Organizations	Y	N	M
Adult enrichment classes			M
Aerobics classes			M
Amusement parks		N	
Apartment bldg. pools & rec rooms			M
Art museums			M
Ballroom dance clubs			M
Beaches		N	
Bicycle group tours			M
Bicycling clubs		N	
Bike paths		N	
Block parties			M
Book discussion groups	Y		
Bookstores with reading area	Y		
Botanical gardens	Y		
Bowling leagues		N	
Bus tours			M
Camping clubs			M
Charities			M

Places, Activities, & Organizations	Y	N	M
Charity and fund-raising events			M
City parks			M
City streets (busy areas)			M
Civic groups			M
Coffeehouses for sitting and reading	Y		
Computer user groups			M
Conservation organizations			M
Country and Western dance clubs		N	
Country clubs		N	
Cross-country ski races		N	
Cruises			M
Dance spots		N	
Dog owners and breeders clubs		N	
Dog shows		N	
Downtown celebrations			M
Environmental groups			M
Equestrian clubs		N	
Ethnic clubs			M
Festivals (music, beer, seasonal, etc.)	Y		
Folk dancing clubs			M
Food courts			M

Places, Activities, & Organizations	Y	N	M
Foreign language clubs			M
Gambling casinos		N	
Gardening clubs		N	
Golf courses		N	
Health clubs			M
Hiking	Y		
Historical museums			M
Historical societies	Y		
Homeowners associations			M
Horse races		N	
Ice rinks			M
I.Q. clubs		N	
Lectures	Y		
Libraries			M
Motorcycle clubs		N	
Natural history museums			M
Outdoor adventure tours			M
Outdoor clubs	Y		
Overweight singles clubs		N	
Parent organizations		N	
Parent/school organizations		N	

Places, Activities, & Organizations	Y	N	M
Parties	Y		
Playgrounds		N	
Poetry reading clubs	Y		
Political organizations			M
Professional clubs of various types	Y		
Professional singles clubs			M
Public speaking clubs			M
Recreational vehicle clubs		N	
Recreation centers			M
Religious organizations		N	
Resorts		N	
Roller skating rinks		N	
Runs and triathalons		N	
Sailing clubs		N	
Self-help and therapy groups	Y		
Shopping malls		N	
Single parents clubs		N	
Singles bars		N	
Singles support groups		N	
Ski clubs			M
Ski resorts		N	

Places, Activities, & Organizations	Y	N	M
Soccer clubs		N	
Social mixers	Y		
Softball teams		N	
Swimming clubs		N	
Tall clubs		N	
Tennis clubs		N	
Theater groups		N	
Touch football teams		N	
Travel clubs	Y		
Volunteer organizations			M
Widows and widowers clubs		N	
Zoos		N	
Other:			
Other:			
Other:			
Other:			
Other:			
Other:			
Other:			
Other:			
Other:			

because they cover interesting topics and because many of the students are single. Adult enrichment classes are given by profit-making businesses, city parks and recreation departments, and colleges and universities.

The classes given by "for profit" businesses often have the best potential for meeting men because many of their classes are tailored to singles. An adult enrichment class business in our city offers between three and four hundred classes each quarter. Its free catalogs are distributed in stands outside of supermarkets, coffee shops, and singles gathering places.

Call your city government and local colleges and universities to see if they offer adult enrichment classes. The phone numbers of colleges and universities can be found in the yellow pages under "Schools—Academic—Colleges and Universities."

One advantage to meeting a man in an adult enrichment class is that the two of you will probably have an interest in common (the subject of the class). Stephanie met a man in an adult enrichment class who shared one of her interests:

> I have always enjoyed traveling, and I also enjoy writing (I do a lot of writing at work), so when I saw a class on how to become a travel writer, I figured that class was for me. I thought travel writing would be a great way for me to pay for my trips, so I signed up for the class. I liked the looks of one of the men in the class, so during the break, as he was getting a cup of coffee, I said to him, "Are you going to become a famous travel writer?" That simple icebreaker changed my life. One year later we were traveling in Central America together. Although neither of us has become a travel writer, we both now have a traveling companion.

Yellow Pages

It might sound strange to use the yellow pages for finding places to go to meet a man, but they are in fact a good source of ideas. In the yellow pages you will find everything from adult enrichment classes to zoos.

Weekly and daily papers, adult enrichment class catalogs, and the yellow pages are all rich sources of information about places where you can meet single men. To give you an idea of how rich in information these sources are, in Appendix D we have summarized what we found when we checked out these four sources in our area. A glance through this appendix shows that there is a great variety of places, events, classes, and organizations from which you can choose. So how do you know which ones to choose? It is usually a combination of your interests, the number and type of men at a given place, and how easy it will be to meet a man there. Following are some pointers to help you to choose. We give pointers for:

♦ Specific places you can go
♦ Events you can attend
♦ Adult enrichment classes you can take
♦ Organizations you can join

Choosing a Specific Place

Say you want to check out a coffeehouse or city park to see if it is a good place for meeting men. Probably the easiest way is to visit the place and see for yourself. Often one visit will be enough. If it is a commercial business, such as a coffeehouse, you might call and ask a few questions, such as: Does it have musical entertainment, poetry readings, or other special events? What is the age range of patrons? Which nights are busiest?

When you visit a place, notice how easy it would be to strike up a conversation. For example, many coffeehouses and food courts have areas crowded with tables and chairs. At such places it would be easy to strike up a conversation with a man at the next table. Places such as art shows and bookstores also are good because you can move around to see who is there and then get close to any man you want to meet.

Choosing Events

Picture who will be attending. Will the event be mainly for couples, or will there be unattached men there? For instance, a "home show" may attract thousands of married couples, but chances are that few single men would attend. A downtown street fair would attract many single men as well as couples. A boat show will probably have a better ratio of men to women than a craft fair. Some events appeal to a wide range of ages, others a narrower range. For example, a punk rock concert will attract younger men than a big band concert.

Choosing Adult Enrichment Classes

There are several factors you can consider when choosing a class to attend. A class that is interesting to you is an obvious choice because you will have something in common with any man whom you meet in the class. A class that has a large number of men, or more men than women, is also good. You can usually get this information by calling the school and asking how many men and women are signed up for a particular class. Many adult enrichment schools are glad to give out this information.

Some classes are specifically for singles. Classes on dating etiquette, how to flirt, and how to meet the opposite sex are sure bets for finding single men. Although these classes may have more available men, they also may have more available women (i.e., more competition).

Consider whether the social setting of a class will allow you to mix and mingle. Will it be easy to approach men and talk with them? Lecture classes where you have a only a few minutes to meet a man before the class, during the break, and after the class provide limited opportunities. A class such as "Cooking for One," where you do some activity in class, would probably provide an opportunity to talk with every man there. A tour of historic sites in your city or an evening tour of unique bars would also provide plenty of socializing opportunities. Meeting men would be easy on such a tour because you would be constantly mingling with the others in the group. It would probably be difficult not to meet all the men there.

Choosing Organizations to Join

When choosing an organization, it is usually easy to determine the makeup and characteristics of the organization—just call the organization and inquire. Ask how many single men and women are members, and ask about the average age. Also inquire about the rate of membership turnover. A high turnover gives you more opportunities to meet men. It is also a good idea to ask whether you can attend one of the group's activities before you join. If not, see if it has a money-back guarantee.

All of these factors will help you decide where to go to meet a man. There is another decision that is even more important however: You simply must decide to go out. We believe in the fundamental principle that "if you want to meet a man, going out is always better than staying home."

One Sunday Ginger made a decision to be out, and it paid off. Here is what she told us.

My normal routine on Sundays is to go to church and then go home and read the Sunday paper. I realized that I wasn't going to meet any men at my house, so after church one Sunday, I changed my routine. Instead of going home to read the paper, I took the paper with me to a popular downtown coffeehouse. Five minutes after I sat down, this man came up to me and said, "From the back, you look familiar. Were you at the Presbyterian church on Harrison Avenue a little while ago?" He said that he had been sitting several rows behind me and remembered my hair and coat. I invited him to join me for coffee and we hit it off. We have been going together for two months now.

If you are in the habit of staying home, try a different routine. Read the entertainment weeklies and the entertainment sections of your daily paper. Look at adult class catalogs or the yellow pages to find places to go where you will have a chance to meet a man. You will probably find more things to do that are fun, interesting, and educational than you ever imagined. The more you are out *anywhere*, the better.

7

How to Meet a Man in Your Daily Life

*I*magine that you are pushing your cart down a supermarket aisle and you see an appealing man coming your way. You give him a nod and a little smile, and he does the same in return. You steal another look as he passes—he is still smiling. Even though you are interested and he seems interested, nothing happens. You both just keep walking. You feel a little disappointed and wonder about the opportunity you missed.

Such encounters don't have to end this way. There are ways to take advantage of such chance opportunities and get to know a man. You can also increase the number of such opportunities. Here are six ways to improve your odds of meeting the man you want while going about your usual daily activities.

1. REALIZE IT CAN BE DONE

When you go to a singles dance or singles mixer you are probably geared up mentally for the possibility of meeting a man. When you run your daily errands, however, you might not give much thought to this possibility. Because you are not mentally prepared, you may be unaware of many meeting opportunities and as a result be caught off-guard by obvious ones that suddenly present themselves. Being aware is effective because it puts you in the frame of mind to notice meeting opportunities. Don't get so wrapped up in the errand you are running that you fail to notice that interesting man who is nearby.

2. Plan What to Do and Say

It is best to know how you will execute the Five Steps before you arrive at a destination. There is an easy way to do this. On your way, think of the situation you will be in and plan out at least the first three steps: how you will search, how you will get near, and how you will break the ice. Since you will be meeting in a nonsingles situation, planning how to get insurance and extend your time together is also valuable. Having a plan will make you more confident and therefore more likely to take action.

Laurel, a woman who took our class, told us how having a plan helped her meet the man she is now dating.

One day on the way to the supermarket I promised myself I was going to do two simple things. I would keep an eye out for an interesting man, and I would think of something about him that I could comment on to start a conversation.

I ended up in the checkout line in front of a man who was wearing a backpack. I thought for a couple of seconds and then said, "Did you ride your bike to the store?" This got us talking. After I got checked through, I turned to him and said, "I enjoyed talking to you, Curtis. I hope to see you again sometime." With that, I gave him a big smile and went to my car. I waited a few minutes, hoping he would come out. When he didn't, I started driving away, but just then he came running out of the store and waved. When I rolled down my window, he laughed and said, "That was a close call. I wanted to talk to you again, but every octogenarian in the world got in my way as I ran out of the store. I almost missed you." We talked for a few minutes and he asked me out.

Laurel's experience shows that doing only a couple of the Five Steps can lead to success. Next time before you run an errand, plan how you will do at least the first few steps at the place you will be. Having a plan makes you more likely to take some action.

3. ALWAYS SEARCH

If you were at a mall and had some spare time, you could spend time doing the first of the Five Steps, the Search Step. You could wander through all the stores and stroll the length of the mall seeing if you could create a meeting opportunity. Many times, however, you will not have time to kill. When this is the case, do a minisearch: Simply look around and see who is nearby.

For example, suppose you are at an airport waiting for your flight. Before you take a seat in the waiting area, look around to see if there are any men you would like to meet. If you see a prospect, take a seat within speaking distance of him. Since you are going to sit somewhere, it might as well be where you will have a chance to meet someone interesting.

Searching is important. It makes you aware of the opportunities around you and makes you less likely to be caught off-guard.

4. VARY WHEN AND WHERE YOU GO

By varying the time and place of your daily activities, you will see more new faces. If you eat lunch in the same restaurant at eleven-thirty every day, try eating at twelve-thirty some days, or try eating at a different restaurant. You will see a whole new crowd of people. If you work out at noon every day, vary your routine and occasionally go after work. If you usually eat breakfast at home, eat in a restaurant once in a while. If you normally drive to work, try the bus.

Every time you change your routine, you will see new faces. Ellen developed a way to vary her routine to make the most out of what some would call a bad situation—eating alone.

After my divorce, I gave up on the domestic stuff, quit cooking, and got carry-out to eat at home most nights. This routine was boring and lonely. After a while, I changed my routine and started eating out. At most of the places I went, I noticed a fair number of men also eating alone. Eventually, I figured out how to meet a man who is eating alone.

I always choose a place where I can seat myself, such as a cafeteria, salad bar, or food court. Before I take a seat, I look for a man eating alone. When I see such a man, I simply walk up to his table and say, "Would you like some conversation while you eat? I *hate* eating alone." I get a "yes" about half the time. I then have company for dinner and a chance to get to know someone. Of the dozen or so men I have had dinner with this way, two have asked me out. Even when I don't end up with a date, it's still more enjoyable than eating alone.

Think of how you could change your daily routine and bring new people into your life. A simple change can result in a big payoff.

Tip: *When eating dinner out, look for a man reading a book. This is a sign that he has time to kill and may be open to some company.*

---

5. Develop Expertise at Places You Frequent

When you go to the same place frequently, you have an opportunity to develop expertise at that place. You can come up with a plan for how to execute the Five Steps, try your plan, analyze your results, modify the plan, and try it again. After a while you will have a plan that works. Sandra decided that since she goes to the supermarket a lot, it was a good place for her to develop expertise.

Last year a man accidentally crashed his cart into mine in the supermarket—at least I think it was an accident. I suppose he could have done it on purpose, I don't know. Anyway, he apologized, and after we talked for a few minutes, he asked me out. We ended up going together for a few months.

That incident made me realize that the supermarket has possibilities as a place to meet men. Now I no longer wait for men to crash their carts into mine. I take the initiative to make something happen. Since I am only five feet tall, I use my short height as a way to meet men. When I see a man I want to meet, I position myself in the aisle he is coming down and then, when he gets near, I ask him to get something off the top shelf for me. That's usually all I need do. We talk and sometimes I get asked out. I've met several men this way. I've also bought a lot of stuff I don't need.

Sandra still leaves it up to the man to complete the Five Steps. It is our suspicion that she has missed opportunities by waiting for men to ask her out. Even if they have a conversation started in a supermarket for them, many men won't have the experience or nerve to ask a woman out.

Ginny, a student of ours, likes to go to lectures and slide shows and has developed expertise at meeting people at such activities:

I have been to many lectures where there were lots of men in the audience. None ever asked me out until I found a way to help things along. Here is what I do. Before taking a seat, I watch for an appealing man arriving alone. After he sits down, if there are several empty seats beside him, I sit two seats away and say something like, "This should be an interesting lecture. Where did you hear about it?" Then, assuming our conversation is rolling along, I will slide over one seat so I am right next to him. If there is only one empty seat next to a man, I say, "Is this seat taken?" That opener tells me if he is waiting for someone, and when he is alone, it lets me sit next to him without feeling awkward. With either method, I end up sitting next to a man for the entire lecture. It is easy to talk in that situation, and meeting for another lecture is a natural suggestion for getting together again.

6. Practice Striking Up Conversations With Strangers

If the thought of striking up a conversation with a man you find appealing frightens you (as it does many women), there is an easy way to help overcome this fear—practice starting conversations. Make it a habit to say something to people around you as you go about your daily activities. Don't limit yourself to speaking just to those men who interest you. The idea is to develop confidence by talking to *any* man or woman who is near you. The more you speak to people who do not interest you romantically, the easier it will be to start a conversation with a man who does. This practice is a painless way for you to change into a person who can easily start and carry on conversations with men you don't know.

Just going about your everyday routine, you have meeting opportunities. Take advantage of these opportunities and tip the odds of meeting the right man in your favor.

8

Help for Single Moms

*I*f you are a single mother trying to find a man to share your life, the chances are you face two problems: finding a man who is open to a ready-made family and finding the time to look. The "no time" problem is especially acute for single moms who have full responsibility for their children and receive little or no help from their former husbands. Judy made this point clear when she told us what life was like when her children were small.

> I got married when I was seventeen. By the time I was twenty I had three little ones and no husband. Arnold moved out after my third baby was born and never provided a dime in support, or any of his time. My parents helped all they could, but money was still short all the time. There were days when all we had to eat was oatmeal. Those were tough times for me: working at low paying jobs, paying day care expenses, and all that. I wanted a man in my life in the worst way, but had no time to look. I went twelve years without a date.

There is a way to solve the "no time to look" and "finding a man who will accept children" problems simultaneously. Make your time do double duty by looking for a man while you are enjoying activities with your children. Get your kids away from the TV and take

74

them places where there will be other children (and single dads). You will be spending time with your children, and any man you meet will probably have children and therefore be more open to a woman who has children. Here are some suggestions for places to take your kids:

Amusement parks	Hiking clubs with family
Beaches	activities
Bike paths	Libraries
Campgrounds	Museums
Children's concerts	Parks with playgrounds
Children's museums	Restaurants with playlands,
Children's theater	video games, or clowns
Church activities	School activities
City zoos	Single-parent clubs with family
Company picnics	activities
Fairs	Swimming pools
Fun centers in malls, etc.	

After reading this list, Kay, a single friend of ours, said, "The zoo? Go to the zoo to meet a man? Is this some kind of a joke? You've got to be kidding!" We aren't kidding—far from it. We did a survey at our city zoo one Sunday and found about as many dads alone with their children as moms. Although there are single dads at the zoo and other family-oriented places, because such places aren't usually thought of as singles meeting places, few men will make a conscious effort to make contact with you (or any other woman).

To have a good chance of meeting a man, you have to do more than just be there—you will probably have to put some effort into making contact. That is what Janice did one day when she took her daughter to the park near her home in Kansas City.

There are books for women on how to meet a millionaire. I never read any of them, but I'll bet the way I met Marty hasn't been covered. I met my millionaire on a playground.

Before I met Marty I was pretty unhappy. Being single and raising a young child was not my idea of fun. I wanted to be back in a family that was whole, so I did what I could to find a good man. In addition to going to singles functions at church, I took Melissa to places where there might be single fathers with their children.

I got lucky one day last summer at the park near my home. As soon as Melissa and I got to the park I noticed a man pushing two little boys on the swings. I led Melissa over to the swings, helped her get on, and started pushing her. Then I said to the man, "Do you live around here?" That's all I had to say to break the ice. The conversation took off, and before long I felt there was chemistry between us.

It turned out that Marty and his kids live in Laguna Beach, California, and were in town visiting his mother. We saw a lot of each other that week. Most summer romances end when the vacation is over, but not ours. Marty and I have been seeing each other every weekend since we met; either he flies to Kansas or I fly to California. All this flying will end when we get married in June. Melissa and I will be moving to Laguna Beach.

Janice said she "got lucky one day" at the park, but was it really luck? In hunting circles there is a saying, "A good hunter makes his own luck," and that's just what Janice did. She had a plan for meeting a single father, and she followed her plan. She went to places where a single father might be, and when she saw a man she wanted to meet, she got near him and started a conversation. As often happens, she didn't have to do all of the Five Steps. After she got a conversation started, he took over and did Step 5—he asked her out.

Tip: *A park can be a great place to meet a single dad with young children, but not just any park. Some parks, with facilities such as tennis courts and jogging paths, cater to adults. Others cater more to young children and have swings, slides, and swimming pools. To find the parks with the greatest potential for meeting single dads who are out with their kids, locate the parks in your area on a city map and then try a different one on each outing.*

When you go to a singles function such as a singles bar, singles dance, or singles mixer, you might assume that most of the men present are unattached and interested in a relationship, and you would probably be right. You can make the same assumption when you see a man alone with children at a zoo, beach, or amusement park. If he were involved with someone, the odds are that this "someone" would be along on such a family outing.

Tip: *Custody agreements often have the father taking his children on a midweek evening, usually Wednesday. Therefore, Wednesday evenings are a good time to find single dads with their children at pizza places and other kids-oriented restaurants. Take your kids out on a Wednesday and check out such places for single dads.*

Be a good mom and spend time with your children. Be good to yourself and use this time to meet someone who can enhance your life. Your time can do double duty.

~9~

Today's Personal Ads
Connecting by Voice Mail

As we were discussing the personal ads in our class, Rita, one of our students, said, "Who on earth would stoop to using an ad in a newspaper! She would have to be pretty desperate, right?" Heather disagreed. She told the class that she had recently placed an ad in an entertainment weekly paper, and she also said that she had attended a party sponsored by the paper for all the singles who had an ad running. This is what Heather said about the party:

There were more than a hundred men and women at the party. When I saw them, I was really surprised. They were not "the seedy and the needy" who are rumored to run ads. They were just an average cut of men and women whom you might see in any social setting.

Personal ads have changed in the past few years. They used to be confined to singles newspapers, and to answer an ad, you wrote a letter addressed to a box number at the paper. Now personal ads have moved into the mainstream, large-circulation daily papers, and the usual way to respond is by voice mail. Personal ads have become an accepted way for singles to meet. The singles we know who use them are not embarrassed about it.

Do today's personal ads work? One woman who obviously thinks so is Yvonne—she teaches a course on how to use the personals. When we asked Yvonne what her own experience with the personals had been, she said:

> When I lived in Boston I met men by walking my two dogs in the park. The park was in an apartment area with lots of single people. When I moved to Denver I lived in a mainly single-family-home area, and I didn't meet any single men while walking my dog, so I tried placing a personal ad. In my ad I talked about my dogs and about how I wanted to meet a man who also liked dogs. I received sixty responses to my ad, met five of the men, and dated one for a year. When that relationship ended, I ran my ad again with almost identical results.

The personals obviously worked well for Yvonne, but we don't want to oversell them. The use of personal ads, as with all the other ways that you can meet a man, probably won't result in instant success. Most women we know who have used the personals didn't find themselves in a long-term relationship as a result of running one ad, one time.

ADVANTAGES OF USING PERSONAL ADS

Advantage No. 1—Personal Ads Can Help You Meet a Certain Type of Man

By placing a personal ad you can reach out to a man with certain qualities and interests. Pauline wanted to meet a man who was intelligent, highly educated, well read, and liberal. She ran the following ad:

> ACADEMICS
> Professors and other erudite men attract me. This cute gourmet cook, 41, loves Shakespearean festivals, theater soirees, ethnic cuisine, travel, long romantic hikes, and reading together by the fire. Seeking divorced best friend/lover. You will be delighted we met.

Pauline also read the personal ads placed by men, and when a man described himself as a professor, or as intelligent, well educated, or well read, she would usually answer the ad. Over the next several months Pauline met many educated, intelligent men, including thirty professors. Who knows how many years it would have taken her to meet thirty professors by going to singles events? The personal ads enabled her to target the type of man she was looking for.

In addition to helping you find a man with certain characteristics and qualities, personal ads can also target a man who is interested in a certain type of relationship. If your goal is to get married and raise a family, you can state that in your ad, and look for a man's ad with that stated goal. If you are taking a one-year sabbatical to see the world and want a traveling companion, the personal ads may help you find a man interested in such an adventure.

Advantage No. 2—You Can Reach Once "Unreachable" Men

The personals allow you to reach a larger group of men: those who don't go to singles places or attend social events where people normally meet. There may be many reasons for this.

They may have demanding professional lives or child-rearing obligations that leave them little time. Perhaps they are new in town, or maybe they are uncomfortable trying to meet someone in a social setting. In any case, the personals are a way to reach some of these "unreachable" men.

Molly met such a man when she answered the following ad:

> WELL TRAVELED
> Fit professional, 48, likes books, operas, plays. Seeks
> articulate, intelligent lady 35–48 who enjoys same
> for fun, conversation, travel.

The "Well Traveled" and "Fit professional" caught Molly's eye, and she responded to the ad. Her response resulted in a date with an international investor who spent much of his time in Europe on business. He had little opportunity to attend singles events to look for a companion. For Molly, he was reachable only through the personal ads.

Advantage No. 3—You Can Learn a Lot About a Man Before Agreeing to a Date

When you use personal ads, the initial communication between you and the man is usually by phone. A friend of ours who uses the ads told us how valuable she finds the initial phone conversation:

> When a man answers my ad, I talk to him on the phone for a long time before I agree to meet him—sometimes for over an hour. It's amazing how much I can learn about a man in an hour. I ask him questions about everything that's important to me. I even ask about his drinking and drug use. Somehow it's much easier to ask personal questions on the phone than it is when you are talking in person.

Advantage No. 4—You Can Use Personal Ads When at Home or at the Office

Personal ads can be helpful if family or work obligations make it difficult to attend activities and events where you might meet a man. You can read ads, leave voice mail responses, place ads, and retrieve the responses to your ad all from your home or office, and at a time that is convenient for you.

Advantage No. 5—Personal Ads Fit Into a Campaign to Meet Mr. Right

If you are on an all-out campaign to find your man, personal ads can fill any "dead time" you may have. Donna is a nurse who is on just such a campaign. Here is how she uses the personal ads:

> As part of my campaign, I attend lectures, take adult classes, and go to many singles activities. In addition, I have an ad running continuously. For me the personal ads are like a campaign

within a campaign, because I fit them in when I have nothing planned on my activity calendar.

My ad is very narrow in its appeal, so I get just a few responses each week. If a man sounds interesting, I call him when I have some spare time. If I am still interested, I arrange a date at a time convenient for me—usually it is for lunch, Sunday brunch, or a drink after work. The personal ads allow me to make good use of nearly all my time.

Advantage No. 6—Personal Ads Can Help if You Are Isolated From Metropolitan Areas

If you live outside a metropolitan area and have few opportunities to meet single men in social situations, a personal ad might help. With a personal ad you may be able to reach a large number of men—those in any nearby large metropolitan area as well as those in smaller cities. You might be surprised at how far a man will be willing to drive to meet you.

Advantage No. 7—Personal Ads Can Get You Started

If you haven't been on a date in years and you don't know what to do or say, the personal ads are a way to hone your social skills. They will get you used to getting out of the house and meeting men (consider it practice if you like). And while you are "practicing," you might meet just the man you are looking for.

DISADVANTAGES OF USING PERSONAL ADS

Disadvantage No. 1—It Is Difficult to Tell Whether There Will Be "Chemistry"

After you have read a man's ad and talked with him on the phone, you will probably know his age, where he lives, his interests, his religion, and what he does for a living. He might meet all of your requirements, and he might sound wonderful on the phone, but when you talk with him face-to-face you might realize in only a few minutes that he is not for you because you don't feel any spark or chemistry. For this reason, many women don't like using personal ads. In a normal face-to-face meeting situation, you talk with a man and then arrange a date, so you know if there is chemistry *before* you go out with him. When you meet a man using personal ads, you go out with him first and *then* find out whether there is chemistry.

Disadvantage No. 2—Using the Personal Ads Can Be Time-Consuming

Previously we listed as an advantage the fact that you can use the personals in your "dead time." This doesn't change the fact, however, that meeting a given man through the personal ads might require a significant amount of your time.

In one of our classes we discussed how long it usually takes after you meet a man before you know if you would like to date him. Some women thought a ten-to-twenty-minute conversation would be long enough. One woman said she would know within three minutes. Hearing that, another woman said, "I know within three minutes whether I want to marry the man or not." This may be a bit extreme, but it does make a point. It doesn't take long after meeting a man face-to-face before you know whether you are interested in dating him.

When you use personal ads, you often invest several hours of your time before you can finally have that all important face-to-face conversation. Before you meet a man, you must:

♦ Write and place an ad (or read ads)
♦ Listen to his voice mail message (or leave a message)
♦ Talk with him on the phone
♦ Drive somewhere to meet him
♦ Stay for the coffee, drink, lunch, or whatever else the meeting entails
♦ Drive home

Using a personal ad, you could easily spend two or three hours on each face-to-face meeting. Some women feel that this is an ineffective use of their time. Such women say that in two or three hours at an event such as a singles mixer they could talk face-to-face with not one but several men and find out if there is an attraction.

Disadvantage No. 3—Cost

The cost of placing an ad varies with the publication and the length of the ad. Because a publication makes money when people call its 900 number to answer ads, it is advantageous for the publication to have a large number of ads running. To encourage people to run ads, some publications offer incentives (a given number of free words, or free ads). Ask about any specials when you place your ad.

When you answer ads using a 900 number, you are charged a certain amount per minute. You pay for the following:

- ◆ The time it takes to hear the standard pre-recorded instructions
- ◆ The time it takes to listen to the man's voice mail message
- ◆ The time it takes to leave your voice mail message

Gloria had this to say about the expense:

I have an ad running almost continuously. It doesn't cost much because the paper quite often has specials for free ads. However, I once answered three ads and almost fell over when I got my phone bill and saw the $32 charge. I don't think I will do that again. I don't have that kind of money.

You will have the best chance of success by both placing and answering ads; however, you will have to decide whether you can afford to do both. Call the publications in your area and inquire about the typical costs for placing and answering ads.

Disadvantage No. 4—Possible Embarrassment

An old song tells of a restless married man who places a personal ad seeking a woman who is willing to have a discreet affair. When he meets the only woman who responds, she is his wife.

Of course, that's just a song; however, embarrassing and awkward situations occur in the real world too. Helen can attest to that:

> I agreed to go for a bike ride with a man who answered my personal ad. I was embarrassed the moment I saw him, and I think he was too. The night before, he had danced with me at a singles dance. At the end of the dance he said, "Thank you," and walked away. I could tell by the way he said it that he was not interested in going out with me. Having a date with him after he rejected me was weird, and a waste of my time. After the ride, he left without suggesting another date.

Meeting a man through a personal ad whom you already know might be a problem. Having someone recognize you in an ad might be another source of embarrassment. There is a slim possibility that someone might read your ad and recognize you from the way you describe yourself. If you place an ad that gives your age, weight, height, hair color, and profession, you may go to work and have someone say, "Hey Mary! I saw your ad." Some women would find this funny; others would be horrified. Some women write vague ads because they don't want their friends or relatives to recognize them from the description in the ad.

Although embarrassing situations can occur when using personal ads, the majority of women we know who have met men through personal ads do not consider it an issue. Few have had any embarrassing experiences.

Disadvantage No. 5—Dishonesty and Deception

During one of our classes we asked a woman who had used the personal ads whether it had been a positive experience. She replied:

> Hardly! Men are a bunch of liars. They lie about their looks; they lie about their age; they lie about their weight; they lie about their profession; and they lie about being single. They lie about everything.

Another woman in the class had an entirely different experience. She said:

I have gone out with several men I met by answering ads. Every one of them seemed to be honest in their ads. If anything, their ads downplayed their desirable characteristics.

Different women have different experiences. If you do meet a man who fudged a bit in his ad, shaving a few years or pounds, try to be understanding—it is a very human thing to do.

Placing Ads

You can usually find personal ads in weekly entertainment papers that cater to singles, as well as in the major daily newspapers. If you have an interest in a certain activity or hobby, check out the magazines on that subject to see if they carry personal ads. We know a woman who wants to meet a man who shares her great interest in literature. She recently placed a personal ad in a national literary magazine, and so far has received replies from three men, one of whom is about to fly six hundred miles to meet her.

To place an ad with most publications, you provide the text of your ad and record a voice mail message for the men who answer your ad. Your ad will have an identification number, not your name or phone number. A man responding to your ad will call a 900 number, give your identification number, listen to your voice mail message, and leave a voice mail message for you. His message will include his name and phone number. You can then retrieve the voice mail left by any men, and decide which men to call back. After a phone conversation with these men, you can arrange to meet the ones who still interest you.

Publications typically charge a fee for placing an ad that depends on the length of the ad and how many days it runs. You are usually not charged for retrieving your voice mail messages. The man is charged on a per-minute basis for listening to your voice mail and recording his voice mail message to you.

WRITING ADS

There are two parts to your ad: a description of you, and a description of the man you want to meet. The description of you will or will not make men interested in responding. Men are interested in knowing about:

♦ Your characteristics (age, appearance, personality, education, occupation, financial and family situation, and tobacco, alcohol, and drug use)

♦ Your interests (what you like to do and the kind of relationship you want)

The purpose of any ad is to make people want something. Your personal ad is no different—it should make the kind of man you are interested in answer your ad. The description of you and your interests, along with the flavor of your ad, is what will cause men to be interested. A description of the man you want will eliminate some of those who might want to respond. A description of the man you want to meet might include:

♦ His characteristics (age, physical appearance, personality, emotional traits, education, occupation, financial and family situation, and tobacco, alcohol, and drug use)

♦ His interests (the interests you want him to have, and the kind of relationship he must want)

The fewer requirements you put on the man you want to meet, the more responses you will get. A large number of responses might be okay if you have the time to meet a lot of men. If you don't want to run all over town meeting men who might not be right for you, however, write an ad that will limit the responses to just those who are likely to be a good match.

Let's look at an ad and analyze it. The words in italics describe the characteristics of the woman who placed the ad.

BEST FRIENDS AND LOVERS
DWF 46, petite, active, nonsmoker, non-drug-user,
loves dancing, romancing, biking, golfing, the
ocean. Seeking SWM 45–52, emotionally and financially secure, no children, comfortable in jeans or at
black-tie affairs. Can you handle an *independent lady*
and afford to travel?

Although not stated explicitly, by stating that the man should not
have children, she implies that she has no children, or at least no
children living at home. There are some significant characteristics
not mentioned. Her looks, except for being "petite," are not
described, and her education and occupation are not mentioned.
The same ad is shown below, now with the words in italics describing her interests.

BEST FRIENDS AND LOVERS
DWF 46, petite, active, nonsmoker, non-drug-user,
loves dancing, romancing, biking, golfing, the ocean.
Seeking SWM 45–52, emotionally and financially
secure, no children, *comfortable in jeans or at black-
tie affairs.* Can you handle an independent lady and
afford to *travel*?

The title of the ad tells what kind of relationship she wants, and you
also know that she likes to dance, be romantic, bike, golf, visit the
ocean, go to informal and formal affairs, and travel. How about the
man she wants to meet? What does she say about his characteristics?
The words in italics describe the characteristics of the man she wants.

BEST FRIENDS AND LOVERS
DWF 46, petite, active, nonsmoker, non-drug-user,
loves dancing, romancing, biking, golfing, the
ocean. Seeking *SWM 45–52, emotionally and financially secure, no children, comfortable in jeans or at*

> *black-tie affairs. Can you handle an independent lady*
> *and afford to travel?*

Except for age, she says nothing about his physical appearance. Weight, height, occupation, and education do not seem to be an issue. By stating that she is a nonsmoker and does not use drugs, she implies that she is looking for a man who doesn't smoke or use drugs. What does the ad say about his interests? Little specifically, but by stating her interests, she implies that he should like dancing, biking, golfing, the ocean, and travel. Overall she has written an ad that, considering its brevity, is fairly descriptive of what she is like and, with the exception of his physical characteristics, what she is looking for in a man.

There are many ways to describe yourself and the man you want to meet. An ad that is written in a novel or humorous way might stand out from the crowd and entice a man to answer. In contrast to the above ad, the following ad is less definite. It is a unique ad that has more "feeling" and fewer facts.

SIXTIES SWEETHEART
Secure, self-assured, sensible, sensual, strong, stable,
steady, sensitive, seeks similar style with single male.

How does she describe her characteristics? There are a lot of adjectives describing her emotional side and none describing her physical characteristics, except for the implication that she was born in the 1960s. She also has no description of her education, occupation, or financial and family situation, and does not mention tobacco, alcohol, or drug use. The only restriction on the person she wants to meet is that he have a similar style (whatever that means) and be a single male. There are no age or other restrictions. There is no statement describing her interests or the type of relationship desired.

Which of the two ads is better? The one that gets the woman the man she wants. Either one could do the job. The ads appeal to different men. The first ad is more descriptive and functional. The second ad is not very descriptive but has a flavor and feeling that might attract a compatible man.

The following is another ad with flavor and feeling but not much in the way of specifics.

THE FLOWERS

They need to be nurtured, admired, and appreciated. SF, poetic, 34, needs help in this task from a
fellow earthling, 30–45.

Most men we know thought this was a stupid ad. The woman who wrote the ad has a different point of view. She is happily married to the man who answered it.

There is no one good ad for everyone. An ad that works for one person may not work for another. So write an ad that reflects you, your tastes and personality. If it doesn't get the results you want, change it and see what happens. One woman we know changed her ad eight times before she got one that was good for her.

We can't tell you what kind of ad is best for you, but do consider the following advice when writing your ad:

Look at Your Ad From a Man's Perspective

When you write your ad, put yourself in the shoes of the men who will read it. They will decide whether or not to respond based mostly on what you have to offer compared with the other ads, so don't shortchange yourself.

Many ads are badly out of balance, with few words on what is offered and many words about what the ad writer wants. The singles who write these ads seem to be thinking, "Since I am ordering a love partner, I might as well order exactly what I want." They write very little about themselves while indulging a lengthy description of the desired mate. Here is an ad that is badly out of balance:

SWF, 39. You: SWM, 35–45, Over 6', positive, fit,
with brains and good looks, financially secure, cul-

turally aware, flexible, from a happy family, no kids.

When a man reads this ad he learnes only that the woman is a thirty-nine-year-old single white female. This ad is typical of those written by people who are thinking mostly of what they want, not what they have to offer.

Don't Set Yourself Up for Rejection

You probably want to make yourself sound very appealing, which is understandable, but be somewhat realistic. Remember, there will be a day of reckoning when you meet a man who answers your ad. Don't set yourself up for rejection by giving an unrealistic or inaccurate description of yourself. An average-looking forty-two-year-old blonde wrote an ad that started off with, "Scandinavian Goddess." A man who answered her ad arranged to meet her in a restaurant. When she entered the restaurant he was already seated. She said, "When he saw me, I could see his face fall from across the room." It wasn't that she was ugly, but few women can measure up to a man's expectation of a Scandinavian goddess.

Bud, one of our students, has a prosthetic arm as a result of an industrial accident. He said he had tried the personal ads, with no luck. When we asked him about his ad, he said that he had described himself as an athletic man who enjoys hiking and skiing. Bud said the women who answered his ad were obviously shocked when they saw his arm. One woman said, "I thought you said you were athletic. What about that arm?" Because of reactions like this, Bud stopped using the personals.

The personal ads might be a good way for Bud to meet a woman who will accept his prosthetic arm, but they didn't work for him because he had written an ad that left out a detail important to most women. His ad certainly could say that he is athletic, because he is, but he should have mentioned his arm. Certainly that would reduce the number of responses he gets, however, the responses that do come in will be from women who probably do not object to meeting a man with such a handicap.

Write an Ad That Stands Out

The publication you advertise in might have hundreds of ads placed by women trying to meet men. With this kind of competition you don't want an ad that blends in with all the others. In a magazine article on how to write a personal ad, it was suggested that you read the other ads, and then use similar words and phrases in your ad. That's okay up to a point, but avoid using so many of the "standard" words and phrases that you turn into a generic woman. Read the other ads, read your own ad, and then ask yourself: Does it stand out? If I were a man would I answer it?

Use Standard Abbreviations to Save Money

To save money, you can use abbreviations. Publications that handle personal ads often have a list of abbreviations that are standard in their ads. Here are some that are typical:

A	Asian
B	Black
Bi	Bisexual
D	Divorced
F	Female
G	Gay
H	Hispanic
J	Jewish
S	Single
M	Male
NS	Nonsmoker
W	White
WW	Widowed
LTR	Long-Term Relationship

When giving a physical description of yourself, you don't have to be wordy. For example, one way to describe yourself might be:

SWF I have blond hair and blue eyes. I am 40 years
old, 5' 5" tall, and weigh 135 lbs.

That took sixty-one characters (not counting punctuation). This
could all be said as follows:

SWF blond/blue, 40, 5'5", 135 lbs.

That took only twenty-three characters, and there is not much
chance of it being misunderstood. Save your words for the things
that can't be so easily abbreviated.

Frequently Used Terms

Here is a list of words and phrases that are sometimes used in personal ads. They might help you decide how you want to describe
yourself, the man you want, or the type of relationship you want.

Physical Appearance

You	Him	
x	x	athletic build
x	x	attractive
x	x	average-looking
x		beautiful
x		curvaceous
x		curves in all the right places
x		cute
x		easy on the eyes
x	x	fit
x		full-figured
x	x	good-looking
	x	handsome
x		leggy
x	x	nice-looking
x		petite
x	x	physically fit
x		proportional
x		Rubenesque

	x	rugged-looking
x	x	sexy-looking
x	x	tall
x	x	trim
x		voluptuous
x	x	weight proportional to height

Personal/Personality

accomplished
adventurous
affectionate
articulate
athletic
caring
communicative
compassionate
confident
considerate
cosmopolitan
creative
cultured
educated
emotionally secure
emotionally stable
energetic
fit
fun
fun-loving

gentleman
good
good listener
healthy
honest
hopeless romantic
humorous
independent
intelligent
intense
lady
lover of life
loyal
mature
mischievous
nonconformist
optimistic
outgoing
passionate
personable

playful
positive attitude
risk-taker
romantic
sensitive
shy
sincere
sophisticated
spirited
spiritual values
spontaneous
sporty
strong
thoughtful
trustworthy
vivacious
well-traveled
witty
zest for life

Habits

nonsmoker
smoker
light drinker
no drugs

Family Situation

divorced
empty nester
separated
single
single parent

Job/Profession/Wealth

financially secure
financially stable
professional
successful
well-off

Relationship Desired

companionship
companionship, maybe more
friendship first
friendship, fun, activities and everything else
fun-filled
lasting relationship
long-term relationship possible
looking for a committed long-term relationship
looking for a long-term relationship possibly leading to the M-
    word
loving
marriage
meaningful relationship
monogamous relationship
platonic relationship
romantic relationship
someone to have summer fun with
special lover and friend
start with friendship, leading perhaps to marriage and a family
travel companion

What is *not* desired (Note: Some women think that it is better to ask for what you want in a positive way and avoid these negative terms.)

no addictions
no airheads
no attitudes
no beards
no carriers of heavy baggage
no cat lovers

no game players please
no introverts
no mind games
no religious or political zealots
no smokers or dopers
no TV addicts
no unraised children
macho males need not apply

RESPONSES TO YOUR AD

The number of responses you get will depend mostly on the following:

♦ How appealing your ad makes you sound
♦ How restrictive your ad is in what you require in a man and in a relationship
♦ How well your ad is written (e.g. interesting, humorous, appealing, etc.)
♦ The size of the publication's circulation

The largest number of responses we know of were received by a woman who wrote this ad:

PETITE
SWF, 18, shy, pretty, no children, desires older man
for romantic relationship.

Apparently a young, shy, pretty, petite woman with no children is what many men are looking for—this ad received 306 responses. The only restriction on the man is that he be "older." The relationship desired is "romantic," which would interest most men.

The smallest number of responses we know of were received by a fifty-year-old man who wrote the following ad:

ROMANTIC
SWM, 50, would like to meet a slim, attractive
woman in her 20s for discreet romantic adventures.

This ad received only two responses. You might say that two responses is one more than he really needed; however, both responses were from women near his age, and they both scolded him and told him he should go out with women his own age.

Choosing From Your Voice Mail Responses

After you have placed an ad, the fun begins. Men answering your ad will leave a voice mail message describing themselves and giving their phone number. After you listen to the message, about all you can do is see if he meets your qualifications and try to get a feeling for his personality.

Although there are no special rules or guidelines to follow when listening to your voice mail responses, some women do have their own rules. Gloria had this to say about judging voice mail responses:

I used to call nearly all the men who answered my ad, but now I only call the men who leave what I consider to be a positive message: one that has a little enthusiasm and maybe a compliment on my ad. I don't call the men who leave only their name and number, who sound desperate, or who are unenthusiastic. It's been my experience that these men are usually not as appealing or as sophisticated as the ones who leave a better voice mail message.

ANSWERING ADS

It's fun to read through the personal ads to see if one intrigues you. Sometimes, however, you need to read between the lines because it is natural for men (and women) to write ads that put everything in a positive light. Sometimes facts are stretched to the point of misrepresenting the truth, and negative information may be omitted. Age, physical appearance, and financial situation all might be fudged a bit. As mentioned earlier, some women find this to be a problem, others do not. At least you don't have to depend on the information in the ad. Anything that is important to you can be verified when you talk with a man on the phone, and then later when you see him in person.

To respond to an ad, you call a 900 number, enter the identification number of the ad you want to respond to, and leave a voice mail message for the man who wrote the ad. Because you want to make a good impression, and because you will be charged by the minute when you leave your message, it is best to prepare for the call. Preparation is especially important if you are going to answer several ads. Here is one way to prepare:

♦ Cut out the ads that interest you and tape each to a separate sheet of paper. This will separate the ads and the identification numbers from all the others in the paper, which will help prevent a mixup.

♦ On each sheet of paper make an outline of what you are going to say in response to that ad. Leave it in outline form, so you are not tempted to read your response—you want your response to sound natural.

♦ Early in your response, give your first name and a telephone number.

♦ Say something complimentary about the ad. This makes your response more personal.

♦ Give a brief description of yourself and your interests, including your age.

♦ Be enthusiastic.

♦ Repeat your first name and phone number at the end.

Using your outline, practice what you are going to say before you leave your message. It helps to record your message, then play it back to see how you sound. Try to sound relaxed and unhurried.

Some publications have the option of either leaving your own voice mail message or leaving a message in which you answer a set of pre-recorded questions, such as:

♦ Why are you responding to this ad?

♦ What are you like?

♦ What do you like to do in your spare time?

♦ If you go on a date with the person who wrote this ad, what would you like to do?

THE FIRST PHONE CALL

The first time you call the man (if he responded to your ad) or he calls you (if you responded to his ad) you will have a chance to qualify him. Joan used to use the personal ads on a regular basis—that's how she met her husband. She found that talking to a man on the phone before meeting him was extremely helpful. Like other women we know, she found it easy to talk about personal subjects on the phone. She also said that a woman needs to be on her toes during the first phone conversation, because apparently men also feel at ease asking personal questions at this time. Here are some of the questions men have asked Joan (and her replies):

♦ Are you dating? *(I go on dates, but I'm not dating anyone seriously.)*

♦ Why did you place an ad? *(I just thought it would be interesting to try the personals.)*

♦ Do the personals work for you? *(I've met several nice people. It's been a positive experience.)*

♦ How long have you been doing the ads? *(This is a new experience for me.)*

♦ How many calls do you get? *(I guess my ad is kind of narrow because I get just a handful of responses.)*

♦ Why haven't you met someone? *(I think it's normal for it to take a while to meet someone with whom everything clicks.)*

If during this first phone call you decide that you don't want to go out with the man, simply say, "I really appreciate your taking the time to talk with me, but I'm not going to be able to make a date to get together. I wish you the best."

Tip: *Take notes during the first phone call. If the man says he has a new hobby, is going on an interesting trip, or tells you the name of his son, write that down. If you arrange to meet him, review your notes just prior to the meeting to see if there is anything that can be used to start a conversation or to keep it rolling. These notes are also helpful for you to insure he's being truthful.*

THE FIRST MEETING

Although you may be excited about the man you are going to meet because he sounded great on the phone, it still might be best to arrange a short first meeting—your feelings might change after you meet him. If they do, it is better to face a thirty-minute conversation rather than a four-hour evening with a man you don't like.

Lunch is a good first meeting, as is coffee or drinks after work. You could also suggest meeting for breakfast before work or for brunch on the weekend. Meeting for coffee or drinks after work has the added advantage of letting you suggest dinner together if the meeting goes well.

Although there are no hard and fast rules about who pays on these first meetings, a suggestion to go Dutch is almost always appreciated. The man is not courting you during this first meeting; both you and he are deciding if you want to get involved. If you have decided that you would like to see him again and he offers to pay, it would be okay to let him. If you do not intend to see him again, however, he will not be pleased when you let him pay and then tell him that it isn't going to work for you. You can also make the first meeting inexpensive; then who pays is less of an issue.

During this first meeting you have an opportunity to have a good time and learn more about him. The end of the meeting has the potential to be an awkward time. It will be less, so, however, if you know what you are going to say. If you want to go out with him and he does not ask you, you can say something like, "I enjoyed talking with you. Call me and let's go out again sometime." If he doesn't have your number, give it to him at this time. If he asks you out, but you don't want to go out with him, it is not necessary to make excuses or to say anything about the chemistry not being right. Simply say, "I have enjoyed talking with you, but I can't make another date. Best of luck to you."

Safety Considerations

When you answer an ad, you give your phone number to a man you don't know (your voice mail message must contain your number so a man can call you). Some women are uncomfortable doing this.

You can avoid giving out your phone number by placing an ad. Then a man will read your ad, respond by voice mail, and, if he wants to meet you, leave his name and phone number. You can then call him, and he won't have your phone number. If you call a man who has caller I.D., however, he will have your number the moment you call him (to prevent this, ask your phone company to block your number).

Your first date might also be a safety concern. For this reason, many women prefer to meet a man during the day, in a busy public place, and for a limited time.

Having Realistic Expectations

If you decide to use the personals, be realistic about it. You have *not* just tapped an inexhaustible supply of perfect men who will all love to be with you. This is not a great panacea—it is simply one more way to meet men. Try the ads a few times and give them a fair shake. Don't be in a hurry to write them off, as a psychologist we know did. Here is her one experience using the personal ads:

> After my husband died, it took a long time to have the desire and the nerve to meet a man again, but after a year went by, I decided to try. I answered a nicely written personal ad, and we met for dinner. He was a nice man, but he never called back. I won't try that again. The personals don't work for me.

This woman was hurt by the disappointment and rejection, but she was expecting too much from one date. Expecting to find your soul mate when you meet only one man is not realistic. Of course, it can happen, but the odds are not with you and it is best not to expect it. Most likely, some men will reject you, and you will find some men unacceptable and reject them. Many women meet a fair number of men before they find a good match.

There was a woman in one of our classes who was on an impressive campaign to meet her Mr. Right. She was well organized, and she had an activities calendar filled out for each month. This is how the personal ads fit into her campaign:

> I'm taking night school classes, I'm in a church group for singles, I go to singles dance spots, and I go to every singles mixer I can find. I also have a personal ad running continuously, and I read men's ads. I usually get two or three responses to my ad each week. Most of the men I meet through the personals are men I wouldn't meet anywhere else. They don't go to singles dance spots, they aren't in my church group, and they don't go to singles mixers.

Whether or not you will meet the love of your life through the personal ads is impossible to say. But there is one thing that can be said with reasonable confidence: If you decide to use the personals, you are about to have one of life's more interesting experiences.

Part II

Putting Your Plan
Into Action

Some of the women who took our class made little effort to change their ways, and as a result, their ability to meet men did not improve. Others decided to take control of their futures by applying the techniques they had learned in our class, and their ability to meet men *did* improve—it changed their lives. As one of these successful women said, "If you learn how to do the Five Steps, and then do them, you will meet the men you want to meet."

You have the same choice. You can continue to wait for Lady Luck (or your present methods) to bring a prince into your life, or you can take charge and apply our proven methods for meeting the opposite sex. You are not born with the skills and knowledge you need to meet the right man, but you can acquire them. Whether you do or not is up to you. It's your choice.

In the preceding chapters we covered the fundamentals of the Passive and Active Techniques and how to use the personal ads. The next five chapters show how the Passive and Active Techniques can be tailored to five specific places:

♦ A singles mixer
♦ A health club
♦ A bookstore
♦ A singles bar
♦ A running event

We are not necessarily recommending these five places as the best places for you to go to meet a man. You may find that you have more success in other places (anyplace can be good if there are men there and you know how to meet them). We chose these places only to give examples of how the Passive and Active Techniques discussed earlier can be customized to work in specific meeting situations.

The next five chapters are not necessarily meant to be read sequentially; they are intended more as a reference. If you are going to be in one of these five meeting situations, read the corresponding chapter. It will give you a little refresher course on the Five Steps, with specific advice on how to apply the steps at that place. It will also be beneficial for you to read the appropriate chapter before you go to a place that is similar. For example, if you are going to any large social event such as a big party, a convention, or a street fair, read how to meet a man at a singles mixer. The advice on how to meet a man in a singles bar can apply to any event where there will be dancing, such as a wedding reception or singles dance. The advice on how to meet a man at a health club and at a running event may give you ideas that you could apply to other exercise-related activities, such as swimming, skiing, or playing tennis.

❧ 10 ❧

How to Meet a Man at a Singles Mixer

Singles mixers are social events where singles gather to mix and mingle in a cocktail-party atmosphere. Many types of events could be called singles mixers. For example, if attended by a large number of singles, wine tastings, art shows, and wedding receptions could all be considered singles mixers. The advice in this chapter applies to all such places.

The art museum in our city puts on a fund-raiser that can be described as a typical singles mixer. Every Wednesday evening, the museum sets up a portable bar and hires a jazz band. This fund-raiser has caught on as a good place for singles to meet, and most of the people there are single. Six to eight hundred people attend on a typical evening. Even though the atmosphere is similar to a singles bar, many singles prefer the art museum mixer as a way to meet a mate. Telling your mom you met your new boyfriend at the art museum certainly sounds better than saying you met him in a bar.

Advantages of Singles Mixers
Singles mixers attract a lot of men who are single and looking. Mixers held after work near office areas often attract high-income executives and professionals.

Disadvantages of Singles Mixers

On your first few visits you might have difficulty starting conversations with strangers, and you might feel as if you are on display. Some singles mixers have a meat-market atmosphere that can take some getting used to.

HOW TO MAKE YOURSELF MORE APPROACHABLE AT A SINGLES MIXER (THE PASSIVE TECHNIQUE)

Many men have a hard time meeting women at a singles mixer. They go hoping to meet a woman, but spend most of their time standing alone or talking to other men. Their fear of rejection and their lack of skill keep them from approaching women and starting conversations.

Barbara, a friend of ours, made this comment about a mixer she had gone to several times:

> I don't understand the men who go there. They just stand around looking at the women. Sometimes I can tell a man is interested in me, but instead of coming over to talk, nothing happens—he keeps to his friends. I get tired of standing there smiling.

Here are some suggestions for ways Barbara, and you, can encourage these interested men to approach:

Be Alone

We realize that being at a mixer alone is difficult for many women. One woman, when teased that she was always at a singles mixer with her girlfriend, replied, "I know. I only come here because my girlfriend meets me here. In fact, when I got here tonight and couldn't find Martha right away, I got kind of panicky." When we advise women in our class to go to singles mixers alone, some of them look stunned, as if we had asked them to do something totally unreasonable. It takes us a while to convince them that while being with their girlfriends might make them feel more comfortable, it also keeps men from approaching them. If you must go with a friend, don't spend a lot of time with her. The more time you spend there alone, the better chance you have of meeting a man.

Be Both Visible and Accessible

When you arrive at a singles mixer, don't sit or stand in the first convenient spot. Take a few minutes to find a place where men can easily see you and get near you. Here are five things to consider when you are looking for a good spot:

Don't Sit Down

Your best bet is to remain standing. Some mixers have areas with tables, as well as open areas where people stand. The women at the tables are seldom approached. Many men assume that these women are there just for the entertainment and that the ones standing are trying to meet a man. In addition, most men won't approach a woman if they feel they are being watched. Few things make a man feel more conspicuous than weaving between tables to get near you.

Stand in the Right Place

By standing in the right spot, you can increase the odds that you will be approached. A good place to stand is near a high-traffic area where men passing by can easily see you and get near you without feeling conspicuous. For example, if there is dancing, make it easy for a man to ask you to dance by standing near the dance floor.

Most men prefer making an indirect approach by getting near you first and then, a short time later, casually saying something. Only the experts are good at the direct approach of walking up to a woman and immediately starting a conversation. To make an indirect approach easy for men, avoid standing in the middle of an open area away from other people. When you are isolated from the crowd it is difficult for men to stand near you without immediately speaking.

Leave Space for a Man

When you are standing, leave a space beside you into which a man can casually move. Then, when he feels the moment is right, he can turn to you with a remark, such as, "Do you like this band?" In a crowded, high-traffic area it's especially critical to leave a space so a man won't block traffic when he stops to get near you.

Don't Form a Closed Circle

If you are talking with a group of friends, don't form a closed circle—this shuts men out. Give men an easy way to approach. Stand in a semicircle so men can easily join your conversation. If you are with only one friend, you and she should lean back against a railing or stand against a wall so you are at least partially facing out. Talk to your friend by turning your head rather than by standing facing her. When you stand facing your friend, you turn your back to men, shutting them out.

Don't Be in the Company of a Man

Some women go to singles mixers with a group from work and spend the evening talking to the men and women they work with. If a man sees you talking to another man, he will assume that you are taken and will not approach you. The same thing holds true if you are just having an interesting conversation with a man you have met at the mixer who doesn't interest you romantically. As long as that man is there, no other man is likely to approach.

Wear or Carry a Conversation Piece

There are many places where it is useful to wear or carry a conversation piece; however, it's especially advantageous at a singles mixer. There are often hundreds of men and women at a singles mixer trying to meet someone, and it is surprising how seldom they do. Many singles will be just standing around, not talking to anyone or talking to friends of the same sex. One reason for this lack of contact with the opposite sex is that so many people are at a loss for words for opening a conversation. Make it easier for men by wearing or carrying something they can comment on.

Many singles mixers are held right after work, and most people come well dressed. Conversation pieces like T-shirts with words are not always appropriate, but a button with words would be okay. The most appropriate conversation pieces include prominent or unusual jewelry, a flashy item of clothing, or an unusual purse.

Some women are well aware of how useful a conversation piece can be. One woman at a singles mixer said, "I always wear my ankle bracelet when I go out. It's amazing how many men use it to start a conversation."

Make Eye Contact and Smile

It is important to encourage men by making eye contact and smiling. At a mixer there might be many women whom a man would like to approach, but his fear of rejection could be keeping him from taking any action. Your smile sets you apart from the crowd and lets him know that among the dozens or hundreds of women there, you are open to being approached by him.

Don't Wear a Ring on Your Wedding-Ring Finger

Most men will check for a wedding ring before approaching a woman at a mixer. To avoid confusion, don't wear any ring on your wedding-ring finger.

The above suggestions will help men overcome their fear and increase the odds that they will approach you. Rather than trying to help men get up the nerve to approach, however, take the initiative yourself in the meeting process by using the Active Technique. It puts you in control and enables you to meet the men you find appealing.

How to Use the Five Steps at a Singles Mixer (the Active Technique)

The Active Technique, where you take the initiative to meet a man and arrange a date, is the most effective technique to use at a singles mixer. Once you master the Active Technique, you will enjoy the control it gives you in determining whom you are going to meet. Here's how to apply the Five-Step Active Technique at a singles mixer:

Step 1—Search

When you arrive, you might be faced with a crowd of hundreds. Although such a large crowd can be intimidating, it also provides many opportunities to meet men. To take advantage of these opportunities, you have to actively search to find the man (or men) you want to meet. For most people, the search step is the easiest of the Five Steps.

There are two main search strategies that work well at a singles mixer. Either stand near a high-traffic area and watch men as they pass by, or move from place to place and check out the men in different areas. Standing in a corner talking to a friend is not an effective search. Searching is an active process that requires some concentration.

Tip: *Searching at a singles mixer makes many women feel self-conscious. They think everyone is watching and knows what they are doing. If you were searching through the crowd trying to find your girlfriend, though, you wouldn't feel conspicuous. Therefore, pretend you are searching for your girlfriend and nobody will know the difference.*

Step 2—Get Near

At a singles mixer, the best strategy for getting near depends on where the man is standing and how many people are nearby.

Strategy for Getting Near a Man Who Is Standing Alone, Away From a Crowd

If a man is standing alone in the middle of an open area, both you and he will be uncomfortable if you walk over and stand near him without speaking. In this situation, your best strategy is to walk directly up to him and immediately start a conversation. This simultaneous execution of Steps 2 and 3 is a bold approach, but one worth learning because many situations require it. Icebreakers suitable for this direct approach are given under Step 3 (Break the Ice).

Strategy for Getting Near a Man Who Is Standing in a Crowd

Work your way through the crowd until you are near him, then stop and casually look around while you wait for an opportunity to start a conversation. The more crowded the room, the closer you will be able to get without feeling self-conscious.

Strategy for Getting Near a Man in a Conversation With Others

Try to join their conversation. Stand just outside the group and show an interest in what they are saying. If you stand close and listen with smiles and nods, making eye contact with members of the group, they will usually open their circle to include you. If their conversation has been slowing down and getting dull, they may be eager to include you in the group, hoping you will liven things up.

Step 3—Break the Ice

To give yourself more confidence, plan icebreakers for different situations you might encounter at a singles mixer.

Planned Icebreakers for a Man Standing Alone, Away From a Crowd

In this situation where you must walk up to a man and immediately speak, a self-introduction works well:

"My name is Ruth. Would you like some conversation?"

"Hi, I'm Ruth. How was *your* day?"

"Are you having a good time? I'm a bit overwhelmed by the size of this crowd. By the way, my name is Ruth."

Planned Icebreakers for a Man Standing in a Crowd

If you have been standing near a man for a few minutes, you can casually turn to him and say something like:

"Do you work [live] around here?"

"And what do *you* do?"

"What do you think of this place [event, crowd]?"

"Have you ever been here before?"

Other Planned Icebreakers

When you are planning your icebreaker, consider whether there will be something about that particular mixer you can comment on. For example, if you know there will be a jazz band, you could plan on saying:

"What do you think of this band?"

"Do you know the name of this band?"

"Have you ever heard this band before?"

"Do you like jazz?"

Spontaneous Icebreakers

A spontaneous icebreaker could pertain to the man or to your immediate situation or surroundings. Here are some examples:

"That's a nice suit. What kind of material is it?"

"Did you get caught in that traffic jam on Broadway?"

"This place seems busy tonight. Is it usually this crowded?"

"What kind of job do you have where you can wear a shirt that color?"

These icebreakers are not spectacular, and they don't have to be. What you are really saying is, "I would like to talk to you. Would you like to talk to me?" If the man is interested, any opener will work.

Step 4—Continue the Conversation

After your icebreaker you can chat about the event or some other impersonal topic, but after a few minutes, concentrate on achieving your conversation goals.

Conversation Goal No. 1—Get Insurance

At a singles mixer, many people will be milling about, moving between conversation groups. In this environment, even though you have a conversation started, there's a chance it could get interrupted. This makes it important to get insurance (the man's name and enough information about his work to enable you to call him there) early in the conversation. If you have insurance and the conversation gets permanently interrupted, you can call him the next day and invite him to meet you for lunch. The questions you need to ask to get insurance are just typical questions frequently asked at a singles mixer:

"By the way, I'm Ruth. What's your name?"

or, if you want his first and last names:

"By the way, I'm Ruth Collins. What's your name?"

"Where do you work?"

"What do you do there?"

Once you have this information, you have a chance to reach him if your conversation ends before you have exchanged phone numbers. If you have only his first name, you might be able to reach him at work with the help of the company operator and your knowledge about what he does there. If you have his full name, you can probably reach him at work or find his home number in the phone book.

Conversation Goal No. 2—Qualify Him

It's easy to spend an entire evening having an engaging conversation with a man who is totally inappropriate for you. When this happens, you may be missing an opportunity to meet a more suitable man. To avoid wasting your time, qualify the man to find out if he is right for you. Qualifying a man at a singles mixer is easy because the main purpose of a mixer is for people to socialize. When you ask qualifying questions, he will probably think that you are simply looking for conversation topics. Put him at ease by asking your questions in a casual manner and conversing for a few minutes on each subject before going on to your next question. Draw the conversation out by occasionally telling him something about yourself. Avoid asking questions in a rapid, machine-gun fashion. You don't want the man to feel as if he's being interrogated. You can also get information without asking direct questions; simply bring up a topic of interest to you and see how he reacts.

If you determine that a man doesn't meet your requirements, it's usually best to end the conversation so you can spend your time with someone more suitable. At a singles mixer, breaking off a conversation is sometimes a problem. In a world where people were totally honest, you would simply say, "I don't want to talk to you anymore. I'm going to leave now." Most of us aren't that blunt, however. We prefer to make some kind of excuse or tell a little white lie to escape from a conversation. You could say, "If you'll excuse me, I'm going to circulate a bit; it's been nice talking to you," or, "A friend of mine is supposed to meet me here. I'd better go see if I can find her. It's been nice talking to you."

Tip: An excuse to end a conversation that works well when you have a drink in hand is, "Well, if you'll excuse me, I want to get another drink." If you are going to use this excuse regularly, make your first drink something on ice. Then, after you leave a conversation, partially fill your glass at a drinking fountain. You can use this empty glass excuse frequently and still be in condition to drive home at the end of the evening. With this excuse you do run the risk of having him say "Let me buy you a drink." If he does, a clear response is needed to end the conversation. You could say, "Oh, no thanks, I can get it. Nice of you to offer." Then turn and walk away.

Conversation Goal No. 3—Drop Hints

If you want to go out with a man and want him to ask you out (as opposed to you doing the asking), make it obvious that you like him and enjoy his company. Dropping the right hints will build up his confidence and send him a clear signal that you are interested.

You can also give him ideas for a date by mentioning activities that you enjoy. For example, in a discussion of the theater, saying, "That's supposed to be a good play. I'd like to see it," might be all it takes to get him to ask you to see it with him.

Conversation Goal No. 4—Extend Your Time Together

This is a great way to take a small but important step toward a romantic relationship. For example, you could say:

> "It's awfully noisy in here. Would you like to go to the hotel coffee shop and talk where it's quiet?"

> "I haven't had dinner yet. There's a pizza place across the street. Would you like to join me for a bite to eat?"

> "The Deca Dance Club is right next door. I'd like to see what it's like. Would you like to check it out with me?"

Before you go to a singles mixer, check out the neighborhood for interesting places to eat, dance, or listen to music. When you are trying to extend your time with a man, it's a big help to know of a nearby place to go, preferably within walking distance.

Tip: *If the man turns down your offer to extend your time together, he may still be interested in seeing you again. Perhaps he can't stay because he has another commitment. To find out what his refusal really means, jump to Step 5 and close. For example, if your offer of pizza gets the response, "I'm sorry, I can't make it," respond with, "Would you like to make it another time?" That way you will find out for sure whether or not he's interested in you.*

Step 5—Close

This step is difficult because you are opening yourself up to rejection. Many of the men you meet at a singles mixer, however, will be inexperienced, and a bit flustered when it comes time to ask you out.

The only sure way to find out if a man would like to go out with you, but is afraid to ask, is to do the closing yourself. Use either of the two standard closing techniques at a single mixer.

Close No. 1—Suggest an Activity and Give Him Your Number

For example, you could say:

"I've enjoyed talking to you this evening. If you would like to continue our conversation over lunch sometime, here's my card. Just give me a call."

"It sounds as if we both enjoy ethnic foods. If you would like to explore a new restaurant sometime, give me a call. My last name is Jones. I'm the only Julia Jones in the phone book."

"On Friday I sometimes go to the Pearl Street Pub for happy hour. If you would like to meet me there, give me a call. Here, I'll write down my number for you."

Close No. 2—Ask for a Date

Here are some examples of directly asking for a date at a singles mixer:

"I won't be here next Tuesday—I'm going to a lecture on endangered species in North America. Would you like to go with me? It's at the Natural History Museum."

"Would you like to go to the Battle of the Bands at City Park on Saturday? I could pack a picnic lunch for us."

"Would you like to meet for lunch tomorrow?"

There might be an opportunity to have a date later that same evening. For example, you could say:

"I've been dying to see that Mel Gibson movie at the Plaza Center. Would you like to go with me? We could meet there after I go home and arrange for a sitter."

"Would you like to do some western dancing? We could meet at the Branding Iron in Southwood. The band doesn't start until nine. That should give me time to go home and change."

If he accepts your offer to meet somewhere that same evening, always exchange phone numbers in case a car breakdown or other unforeseen circumstance causes one of you to be unable to make the date.

Rachel, a social worker in her late thirties, took our class and then came to several of our support group meetings. Rachel said that she knew there were a lot of available men at singles mixers and that she wanted to learn how to meet them. She told this story at her first support group meeting:

You told me I should go to a singles mixer alone, and when I tried, I was surprised at how I felt. I walked through India and Nepal by myself and wasn't afraid, but going to a singles mixer alone scared me to death.

I tried going to the mixer at the Regency without my girl-friend. On the way there I was feeling shaky, so I stopped by a liquor store, bought a beer, and drank it in the parking lot. When I got to the Regency, I didn't go to the mezzanine where all the people were. Instead, I took the elevator to the second floor where I could look down at the crowd. When I saw what other women were wearing, I felt underdressed, so I went back to my car and put on the clothes I had worn to work.

After I changed, I went to the mezzanine and waited to see what would happen. I didn't like being there; I felt very uncomfortable. One man kept smiling at me, but I didn't give him any encouragement. I didn't want him. There was another man nearby whom I did want to meet, but he didn't come over. I didn't talk to anyone the entire time I was there. It wasn't much fun.

A week later I decided to try going again. Halfway there I lost my nerve. I went to the movies instead.

Rachel's need for a beer, going to the second floor to watch, and going back to her car to change clothes are all indications of the fear she felt going to this singles mixer by herself. She was more afraid to go to a nearby singles mixer than she was to walk alone through a foreign country. Her story illustrates the emotions many women feel when going to their first singles mixer.

We assured Rachel that her fears were normal and that if she went to the same singles mixer two more times, she would begin to get over her fear, and might even start to enjoy it. When we had dinner with Rachel three months later, she told a different story:

> I have learned where all the singles mixers in town are, and I try to go to all of them. I always go alone. I'm going out much too often to be coordinating every outing with a girlfriend. I've gotten used to going alone, and sometimes have a lot of fun. I tingle a little bit before I go; it's kind of like gambling—am I going to hit the jackpot tonight and meet a man I really like?

On her first visit to a singles mixer, Rachel was afraid and ineffective at meeting men. With persistence, she got used to going and eventually learned how to use the Five Steps to meet men. You can do the same. There are hundreds of men at singles mixers, most of them inexperienced at meeting women. By using the Five Steps you can take advantage of this gold mine of opportunities.

❧11❧

How to Meet a Man
at a Health Club

*H*ealth clubs can be great places to meet men—if you know how. But if you don't know how, going to a club will probably do more for your body than for your love life. Knowing what to do makes all the difference.

Advantages of a Health Club
In contrast to singles bars and singles mixers, health clubs are relatively quiet places where you can meet sober men in a smoke-free environment. Most of the men are trim and fit (check out those exercise outfits!), and lead healthy lifestyles. While some men go to health clubs just to work out, many others go because they are trying to meet a woman. Health clubs are open long hours and nearly every day, giving you plenty of opportunities to meet men while getting a workout.

Disadvantages of a Health Club
The cost of a health club membership is a disadvantage for those on a tight budget. If cost is a concern and the club offers a choice of membership packages, sign up for the minimum package. Extras like use of a tanning booth and racquetball courts aren't necessary if your main purpose is to meet a man.

How to Select a Health Club

Visit several clubs for trial workouts. The perfect club will be a convenient, co-ed, well-equipped facility with a male clientele that interests you. In general, clubs with moderate membership fees attract younger men, whereas expensive clubs attract older, wealthier men. Go for your trial workout when the club is busy and check out both the equipment and the men. Ask several men and women if they like the club and are glad they joined.

Tip: A club that allows you to work out in any of several locations has the advantage of letting you see new faces in different parts of town.

A salesperson might greet you the minute you walk in, stay with you during your trial workout, and then pressure you to join. To reduce the sales pressure, make it clear from the beginning that you are going to try several clubs before joining one.

When to Go and How Long to Stay

If you are trying to meet a man, the best time to go is when it's busy. When it's not busy, you have few men to select from. The busiest times are usually Monday through Friday around noon, Monday through Thursday after work, and during the day on Saturday and Sunday. During the evening on Friday, Saturday, and Sunday, you could fire a cannon in most clubs and not hit anyone. To find out when your club is busy, go at various times of the day and week. Going at different times will also let you see a variety of men. Most men have fixed workout times, and you will never see them if you don't exercise on their schedule.

There is usually a complete turnover in a health club every one to two hours. If you have nothing else to do, hang around and see who else comes in. The more time you spend at your club, the greater the chance you'll meet a man. And besides, think how fit you'll be!

How to Make Yourself More Approachable at a Health Club (the Passive Technique)

Many women at health clubs are in a relationship and are at the club to get a workout, not to meet a man. Having been rebuffed by these women, men aren't sure who wants to be met and who doesn't. This uncertainty makes men at health clubs reluctant to approach women. Here's how you can make it clear you are open to being met:

Be Accessible

Most men avoid walking directly up to a woman and starting a conversation. They prefer the indirect approach where they appear nearby as if by chance, and then say something a little later. Make it easy for them to do this. For example, if you are going to stretch, do it where there is room for a man to stretch nearby. If you have a choice of exercise machines, use one that has an empty machine beside it. If there is a sign-up list for some machines, sign up and then hang around with the others who are waiting for a machine to become available. Spend some time in the Jacuzzi.

Tip: It's easy to carry on a conversation while on stair machines or stationary bikes. It's harder to have a conversation on cross-country ski machines, and because of the motion, it's much harder while on rowing machines.

Do What the Men Do

Most aerobics classes have far more women than men. The exercise machines (stationary bikes, stair machines, etc.) will have about equal numbers of men and women, and the free weights area will have mostly men. Avoid the aerobics class. Not only are there few men there, but during the class it's nearly impossible to talk. If a lot of men are using certain exercise machines, that's where you should be. If you learn to work out with free weights, you will always have men around.

Wear or Carry a Conversation Piece

Men will approach you more readily if they can think of something to say to start a conversation. Wear an exercise outfit that is different or striking. Wear a T-shirt or button with words that a man can comment on. Carry a water bottle or a towel that has words or a picture that will provide him with an icebreaker.

Don't Wear Workout Gloves

If your ring finger is covered by workout gloves, a man won't be able to tell if you are wearing a wedding ring. If he doesn't know, he may not approach. Let him know you are single by letting him see your hands.

Don't Wear a Headset

It's difficult for a man to make a casual opening remark to a woman under the best of conditions. A headset makes a casual opener nearly impossible, thus reducing the chance that a man will try to meet you.

There was a cute young woman in our class who was having trouble meeting men. She didn't go to the typical singles functions, but she did spend a lot of time at her health club. It was baffling to the men in the class why she wasn't meeting men at her club, until she said she always wore a headset during her workouts. When they heard this, several of the men who went to health clubs nodded in understanding and made these comments:

"I won't try to meet a woman who is wearing a headset. I feel as if I would be interrupting her."

"I think headphones are intimidating. I don't like shouting an opener and having everyone know I'm trying to meet her."

"When I see a woman wearing a headset at my club, I assume she's wearing it as a way of saying 'Please leave me alone!' "

Make Eye Contact and Smile

A man can see dozens of women in a nonsingles place such as a health club. Some are available, others are not. Some are interested in him, others are not. Your smile lets him know you are available and interested. Unless you smile, he has no way of knowing.

Using the above suggestions to make yourself more approachable increases your chances of meeting a man; however, you will still meet only the men who have some skill at meeting women. Most men lack this skill and are at the health club hoping for a lucky encounter where they meet a woman by accident, without risking rejection.

When men depend on luck and women use the Passive Technique, nothing happens. This point was made in one of our classes when Tim described what it was like meeting women at his health club:

A year ago I joined a health club near work, partly to get exercise, but mostly as a way to meet women. When I first saw all the women at the club, I thought I had died and gone to heaven.

During my first workout, I ran into a friend from work. I said, "Paul, how long have you been coming here?" Paul replied, "Just over a year." Then I asked, "How many women have you met here?" He replied, "None."

I knew Paul didn't have a girlfriend because he complained about it a lot. So I figured he must be doing something wrong if he could go to this club for more than a year without meeting anyone. But it turned out I wasn't any more successful than Paul. After going to this club several times a week for a year, I didn't even know the first name of one woman at the club. It just wasn't as easy as I thought it would be. People seem to keep to themselves at the club. At the beginning of the year I was working out among strangers, and at the end of the year I was working out among strangers.

There are a lot of men at health clubs just like Tim and Paul. They join the club to meet a woman, but they don't know how to make it happen. Instead they depend on Lady Luck to provide an accidental meeting. Take advantage of this situation. Use the Active Technique to make this "accident" happen.

How to Use the Five Steps at a Health Club (the Active Technique)

If you want to meet an interesting man at your health club, get your priorities straight. Are you there to meet a man or to get a good workout? The best routine for meeting a man is different from the best routine for a workout. Assuming that you are there to meet a man, here's how to do it:

Step 1—Search

The difference between going to work out and going to meet a man starts the instant you walk out of the dressing room. If you are there for exercise, you probably have a set routine. You may go to a certain place to stretch for a few minutes, then perhaps jog awhile. Then you go to an aerobics class or use exercise machines in a certain order. Such a set routine is not the best way to meet a man.

To meet a man, as soon as you come out of the dressing room, walk through the entire club to see who is there. See who is on the jogging track and who is waiting for the aerobics class to start. Check out the weight room, the Jacuzzi, and the exercise machines. If you don't see an appealing man, then begin your workout. Interrupt your workout and repeat the search occasionally to see if anyone new has come in.

You might feel self-conscious walking through the club looking for an appealing man. If this bothers you, move through the club by working out briefly on an exercise machine at one end of the club, then moving to one at the other end. Actually, when you are actively searching, few people will know what you are doing. If you saw another woman walking through the club would you pay any attention or think she was "searching"?

Step 2—Get Near

One obvious way to get near is to do whatever the man is doing. If he is stretching to loosen up, stretch nearby. If he is on the stair machine, use the machine beside him. If he is using free weights, use free weights. If he is in the Jacuzzi, get in the Jacuzzi (a Jacuzzi is an especially good place to meet men because people in a Jacuzzi feel awkward *not* talking to one another). If the club is crowded and an interesting man has signed up for one of the more popular exercise machines, sign up for one of those machines and wait near him until you have an opportunity to speak to him. If there's an attractive man waiting in a group for the next aerobics class to start, join the group and stand, sit, or stretch next to him. If you succeed in starting a conversation with a man before the class, then it might be worth your time to take the class and try to continue the conversation when the session is over.

Tip: Some clubs have one Jacuzzi for men and another for women. A club that has one Jacuzzi that is used by men and women at the same time offers a definite advantage for meeting men.

With just a little practice, getting near becomes an easy step to take, and it greatly increases your chances of meeting a man. Once you are near, a man might take over and complete the Five Steps.

Step 3—Break the Ice

Now that you are within speaking distance, if you are going to meet, one of you has to say something to start a conversation. It pays to have a planned icebreaker ready so you won't have to think of one on the spot.

Jackie told us about the icebreakers she uses to meet men at her health club:

My favorite icebreaker is, "Are you training for the Olympics?" This almost always gets a laugh and some sort of response. If the man just laughs and says, "No," I follow up with, "Well, you must be training for *something*, you're working awfully hard." Men then tell me why they are working out. One said he was a bicycle racer; others were getting ready for ski season, working out to overcome injuries, lose weight, or stay in shape. Their response usually provides me with a topic for continuing the conversation.

I have another icebreaker that also works. I stand by an exercise machine, and when a desirable man walks by, I say, "Are you an instructor?" Since the instructors all have gorgeous bodies, the man is flattered that I have mistaken him for an instructor, and will usually smile as he says he is not. I quickly follow this up with, "Well, could *you* help me? I don't know how this machine works." The man is usually willing to help, and it gives me a chance to introduce myself and chat with him after he explains how the machine works or tries to figure it out himself.

To get a conversation started, almost any opener will do, including spontaneous icebreakers in which you comment on the storm raging outside, how hot, cold, or busy the club is, or how much you like his exercise outfit. Spontaneous icebreakers can be so simple that they border on being stupid or obvious, but it doesn't really matter. For example, when you get on an exercise machine with a TV overhead you can ask, "What's on TV?" and you have a subject to begin a conversation. The important thing is to say *something*.

Tip: *If the exercise machine next to the man you want to meet is broken, you can still meet him. Walk up, look at the machine, and as an icebreaker say, "What's wrong with this machine?" He may not know what's wrong with it, but you don't really care. You are just trying to strike up a conversation.*

On aerobic equipment such as the stair machines and stationary bikes, it is acceptable to strike up a conversation with a man at any time. If he is in the middle of a strength set on a machine or using free weights, however, don't use your opener while the veins are bulging out of his forehead. Wait until he's between sets.

Assuming the man is not doing a strength set, it's usually best to use your icebreaker immediately. Sometimes the longer you delay, the more awkward you feel trying to start a conversation. If he is on an exercise machine, walk up to the machine beside him. As you adjust the weight setting, smile and say, "How's your workout going?" This might get a conversation started that could last through the entire time you are on that machine.

Step 4—Continue the Conversation

A man who is concentrating on his workout may be surprised and tongue-tied when you speak to him. A follow-up question or comment after your icebreaker will allow time for him to change his focus from working out to talking with you. Follow-up questions could be, "How long have you been coming to the club?" "Do you exercise regularly?" or "What do you think of this club?" There is always the possibility that, for any number of reasons, he is not interested in you. If you are not getting some positive feedback after a few opening remarks, say, "Have a good workout," and move on. If he responds favorably, however, continue the conversation, concentrating on your four conversation goals.

Conversation Goal No. 1—Get Insurance

In a health club, it's important to get insurance as soon as possible because it might not be easy for either of you to suggest a date with people listening, and there's a good chance your conversation will get interrupted. If you have insurance, you can call him later. Insurance consists of his name and enough information about his work to allow you to call him there.

There are several ways to bring up the subject of his work. You can say, "I come here to work off my job stress. Is your job stressful?" If you are at your club over lunch hour, say, "What kind of job do you have that lets you get away long enough to exercise over lunch?" Or, "You must work nearby if you can get a workout in over lunch." Follow up with questions about his work until you feel you can reach him there by phone. Keep it light and conversational. He won't know what you're doing.

Knowing his name and where he works enables you to call him with a suggestion such as: "This is Judy. We met yesterday in the weight room at the health club. Do you remember? I was wondering if you'd like to continue our conversation over lunch sometime." Or, "Is this Arnold? Hi! This is Judy. We met at the club last Saturday. I remember you like to play tennis. Would you like to have a match after work sometime?"

Conversation Goal No. 2—Qualify Him

Find out if this man meets your requirements so you can decide if you want to go out with him. In a conversational manner, ask questions about topics important to you or make comments on those topics and get his reaction. In a health-club setting it's easy to ask what else the man does for exercise and then work the conversation into his other interests and activities. If you are not sure he's single, when he mentions an activity he enjoys, you can say, "Does your wife enjoy doing that with you?"

Conversation Goal No. 3—Drop Hints

If you want him to ask *you* for a date, give him ideas for a date by mentioning activities you enjoy. Dropping hints about an athletic activity works well in a health club. For example:

"I also ride my bike for exercise. I just had the shop give my bike its spring tune-up. I'm ready to ride."

"I used to play a lot of tennis, until my tennis partner moved away."

"Racquetball looks like so much fun. I wish I knew how to play."

Conversation Goal No. 4—Extend Your Time Together

Talking to a man in a health club may start to get awkward after a while, and even though you have decided that you are interested in him, it might still seem too soon to close. Now is a good time to suggest something that will extend your time together. This will help you make a smooth transition from a casual conversation to a more romantic encounter. You might suggest an activity that the two of you can immediately do together, such as:

"I was thinking about relaxing in the Jacuzzi for a while. Would you like to join me?"

"I'm going to walk a few laps to cool down. Would you like to join me?"

"After I change, I'm going to stop by the juice bar and get something to drink. Would you like to meet me there?"

The suggestion you make to spend more time with the man might depend on the day and time. For example, if you are exercising right after work, the following offer might get a positive response:

"After I finish my workout I'm going to get a sandwich at the sub shop next door. Want to join me?"

On Saturday, Sunday, or holiday mornings, make a suggestion for lunch:

"Would you like to continue this conversation over lunch? The Bean Sprout is right around the corner. It has great salads."

Step 5—Close

At a health club, as in any other personal encounter meeting, you have the option of using two different closing techniques:

Close No. 1—Suggest an Activity and Give Him Your Number

This closing option works well because there are so many exercise-related activities you can suggest. For example:

"It would be fun to go for a bike ride together. Let me give you my number. I have a card in the locker room I can give you."

"I've been looking for a new tennis partner. If you would like to play sometime, give me a call. My last name is Anderson. In the phone book, it's A. B. Anderson."

"Anytime you want to have a game of racquetball, give me a ring. Let me write down my number for you."

And you can always use the old standby, a lunch invitation:

"If you would like to get together for lunch next week, give me a call. My name is Jane and I'm in the accounting department at National Insurance."

If a man is interested in you, knows you are interested in him, and has your number, the odds are he will call.

Close No. 2—Ask for a Date

You can also directly ask for a date. The chance to have a date with an exciting man may be worth risking rejection. If you succeed, you'll be proud of yourself. If you don't get a date, you'll feel good that you tried. Here are some possible ways to ask:

"I'm going to ride the Highline Canal bike path Sunday afternoon. Would you like to join me?"

"The Summit has a good band this Saturday and I'm planning on going. Would you like to go with me?"

"I have Tuesday night free. Are you interested in playing some racquetball?"

Don't hesitate to ask for a date for that same day. If you like the man, why wait? For example, on weekends and holidays, you can suggest an activity for later in the day:

"I'm going to ride my bike downtown this afternoon. Would you like to go with me?"

If he agrees to the date, exchange numbers and arrange the details of the ride. If he says he is busy, follow up with, "Would you like to make it another time?"

Before you go for your workout, think of activities you could do with a man. If you don't have a suggestion for a date already in mind, you may not be able to think of one when you need to.

There are a lot of single men at health clubs. If you want to meet men while doing an activity that's good for you, a health club is for you. You will have the most success by doing the Five Steps. Every step gets you closer to having a date with a desirable man.

∽12∽

How to Meet a Man in a Bookstore

$\mathcal{A}$ s we have said many times before, when you are out somewhere, you have a better chance of meeting a man than when you are at home. In most metropolitan areas, one place you can go is to a bookstore. Not just to any bookstore, but to one of "today's" bookstores—a bookstore that provides amenities such as chairs, couches, tables, and refreshments. These amenities are changing bookstores into social centers where people go to browse, read, meet friends, listen to authors, and have a cup of coffee or a snack. There will be single men there, and a good atmosphere for making contact. Expand your horizons beyond the singles meeting places. Try a nonsingles meeting place—try a bookstore.

Advantages of a Bookstore
♦ You can search for an appealing man without being noticed.
♦ You have the freedom of movement to get near any man.
♦ It will be easy to have an informal, relaxed conversation (men there are typically not in a hurry).
♦ In larger bookstores, you can spend hours and not feel conspicuous. (Try spending hours in a supermarket—the staff begins to wonder after a while.)

♦ Bookstores often have book signings and book readings that bring in crowds and provide an atmosphere where it is easy to mix and mingle.

♦ A bookstore is a safe, alcohol-free environment for meeting men.

♦ Bookstores are open most days of the year, and often until late at night. If you are on a campaign to meet a man, going to bookstores can help fill in blank spaces on your activities calendar.

♦ Most men in a bookstore will be educated and intelligent.

♦ If you like to read, there is a good chance that any man you meet will share this interest.

Disadvantages of a Bookstore

♦ In general, men there will not be trying to meet women; therefore if something is going to happen, you are probably going to have to make it happen by taking the initiative.

♦ There is a chance that the man you approach will be unavailable (i.e., married or involved with someone).

A small neighborhood bookstore might be good because it may be easier to speak to the other customers than to not speak to them. A large bookstore is also good, however, because there are more men to choose from and because you can comfortably spend hours there without feeling conspicuous. To find bookstores in your area, look up "Bookstores" in the yellow pages. Call several and ask if they have author readings, chairs, tables, couches, or refreshments. This type of bookstore has the desired atmosphere because men there are likely to be browsing and unhurried.

There will be more men in a bookstore when there are more people there in general. One time that is often crowded is when there is a book reading or a book signing.

On a Friday or Saturday night you may be more likely to find unattached men. If a man has a significant other, he will probably be with her on a weekend night. Gina found success in a bookstore on a Friday night. Here is what she told us:

Last week I broke up with my boyfriend and I was really bummed out. After being close to someone, it was hard to face a Friday night at home alone. Instead of sitting around feeling sad, I went to my favorite bookstore and, well, tried to meet a man. It wasn't easy—I was pretty nervous. I went in after dinner, walked through all the sections of the store, and spotted an attractive man in the science section.

Getting up my nerve, I picked up a book next to him, then waited a couple of minutes until a woman standing nearby moved on. When she was gone I said, "Are you finding anything interesting to read?" That little opener did it. We had a half-hour conversation and exchanged numbers before we parted. From now on, unless I have something else to do, I am going to the bookstore on Friday and Saturday nights. I think I am on to something.

In bookstores there will be a constant turnover as people come and go. If you go to a bookstore and don't see a man you would like to meet, just wait a while and see who else comes in (waiting paid off for Gina in the above story). If you have nothing better to do (such as no date or nowhere else to go to meet a man), spend a few hours in the store. In general, the longer you stay, the better your chances.

How to Make Yourself More Approachable in a Bookstore (the Passive Technique)

If you wait for a man to approach you in a bookstore, you could wait a long, long time. Most men in a bookstore will not be there trying to meet a woman. Even if a man notices you and wants to meet you, few men have the skills to make it happen in such an environment. Therefore, we recommend that you use the Active Technique and take the initiative. Even if you do take the initiative and approach men in a bookstore, however, it still doesn't hurt to make it easy for them to approach you. Here are some ideas that could make you seem more approachable:

Be Alone

Most men prefer to meet a woman who is alone, so either don't take your girlfriend to the bookstore with you or split up when you get there.

Make Eye Contact and Smile

This technique works everywhere, and a bookstore is no exception. When you see a man you would like to meet, give him a nice smile. It might encourage him to approach you.

Wear or Carry a Conversation Piece

In a bookstore, a man might see you and want to meet you, but not approach because he doesn't know what to say. A book you are showing interest in might give him just the icebreaker he is looking for. A button or T-shirt with a saying might also give him an idea for something to say. You can even refine this technique in order to meet a certain type of man. For example, in a bookstore you could wear a T-shirt that says, "Hiking is my life's work," and get approached by a man who is a reader, and who also loves to hike. That might sound like an unrealistic "fine tuning" of a conversation piece, but don't be too sure—it just might work.

How to Use the Five Steps in a Bookstore (the Active Technique)

When you use the Passive Technique, you will only meet men who come up to you, and in a bookstore, that will be probably be few or none. Rather than wait for a man to approach, use the Active Technique—it usually results in more success, and you get to choose which man you will meet. Here is how to do the Five Steps of the Active Technique in a bookstore:

Step 1—Search

The object of your search is to find a man who interests you, who is not with another woman, and who is not wearing a wedding ring.

There are three basic search methods in a bookstore: an "entry" search, an "overall" search, and a "targeted" search.

The Entry Search

Couples often go to bookstores together and split up after they arrive. The entry search lets you see right away which men are alone and which are there with a woman. To do the entry search, position yourself near the entrance where you can discreetly watch men as they enter the store. If a man is alone and you want to meet him, follow him (at a distance) until you have a chance to get near him.

The Overall Search

Browse through the various sections of the bookstore, looking at the books and checking out the men. Browsing is what people do in a bookstore, so no one will notice what you are doing.

The Targeted Search

With the targeted search, you search only those areas of the bookstore with books on subjects that interest you. A man you meet in one of these areas is probably going to share your interest. Having an interest in common will give you something to talk about when you first meet, and it might be an interest the two of you can share if you enter a relationship.

Janet, one of our former students, used a "targeted search" in a bookstore one evening, and it turned out well for her:

> I can't believe what I did last night. I had plans to meet my girl-friends for dinner at that restaurant right across the street from Hobby Books. On the off-chance that I might meet a man, I went a few minutes early so I could spend some time in the bookstore. I love photography, so I went to the photography section. There was a nice-looking man there glancing through a book, so I got near him and started looking through a book. Then I turned to him and said, "Isn't this a terrific store?" He seemed surprised that I had spoken to him, but he also seemed eager to talk. When he mentioned that he was new in town, I saw my chance to find out if he was married. I said, "Did your family move here with

you?" He said he was single, so after we had chatted for a couple of minutes and I was getting ready to go meet my friends, I handed him my card and said, "It's been nice talking with you. Give me a call so we can get together sometime." He called today, and we're going out Friday night. Can you believe it?

Step 2—Get Near

Since most people in a bookstore stand and browse, you can get near almost any man you want. Wherever he is browsing, you can browse. Develop a sudden interest in the books near him and you will be near enough to him to say something. If he is sitting on a couch or at a table, find a place near him to sit.

Step 3—Break the Ice

Once you are near, there are many comments about the books or the bookstore that you could make which would seem natural and fit in with the atmosphere. For example, as you are browsing next to him you could say:

"Can you recommend anything?"

"Have you found something interesting?"

"This is a great book. Have you read it?"

"Did you see the illustrations in this book? They're wonderful."

"It sure is crowded [empty] in here tonight."

If he is seated at one end of a couch, you could say, "That couch looks comfortable, is there room for one more?" and follow up with, "What are you reading tonight?"

Tip: Carry a small notebook. If a man recommends a book or author, take out your notebook and write down the information. Later, if you want to close, the paper and pen will come in handy for giving him your number.

Step 4—Continue the Conversation

When you first speak to a man, you might catch him by surprise. His thoughts may be elsewhere and it could take a couple of attempts on your part to get a conversation started. Therefore, after your icebreaker, be prepared with one or two follow-up comments; if he doesn't warm up, say, "Have a nice day," and move on. If you are successful in getting a conversation started, however, don't forget to ask questions and make comments that will help you achieve the four conversation goals. Here are the four goals and their importance in a bookstore.

Conversation Goal No. 1—Get Insurance

It is always a good idea to get insurance in case you fail to close. What could prevent you from closing? An awkward pause in the conversation could cause him to suddenly end the conversation (some men may be prone to a little panic when meeting a woman in such an offbeat place as a bookstore). Or the conversation could get interrupted because he has to leave for an appointment, or a friend of his might show up and interrupt your conversation. There is also a chance that you might chicken out and not close. Whatever the reason, with insurance, you have a second chance. If you have his name and know where he works, you can call him at work, identify yourself as the woman who spoke to him in the bookstore, and ask him if he would like to meet for lunch.

Conversation Goal No. 2—Qualify Him

Qualifying a man in a bookstore is like qualifying a man anywhere else—you want to see if he meets your requirements. Since a bookstore is a nonsingles environment, many women think that it is very important to find out if a man is unattached. When you think about approaching a man in a bookstore you might worry, "But what if he is married? That would be terrible!" That is a valid concern; however, women who have met men in bookstores do not find that to be a significant issue. A man's state of involvement with another woman will often come out in the conversation or in his actions (if he is unattached and interested in you, he will probably make it known). It doesn't hurt to find out if he is unattached, but it is not critical that you do so in the early stages of a conversation. If you do end up approaching a married man, even though you might be embarrassed, he probably won't care that you tried to meet him. In fact, he will probably be flattered!

Conversation Goal No. 3—Drop Hints

It doesn't hurt to let a man know that you are interested in him (it encourages him to ask you out). It can also be helpful to mention activities that interest you (it may give him an idea for a date activity).

Conversation Goal No. 4—Extend Your Time Together

This is probably the most important conversation goal in a bookstore. Standing and talking by a bookshelf might become awkward after several minutes, and you are subject to interruptions. If you say, "Would you like to join me for cup of coffee?" and he accepts, you will be in a comfortable situation to have a relaxed conversation with little chance of being interrupted. The good news is that in many bookstores, you don't have to leave to grab a cup of coffee. In a way, a suggestion to extend your time is a good qualifier. If he accepts your invitation, it probably means that he is unattached and interested in knowing you better.

If he responds to your offer with, "I would like to, but I have to meet a friend in a few minutes," come back with, "Want to make it another time?" Then you will find out for sure whether he is interested in you or not.

Step 5—Close

You might not have to worry about closing. Once you get a conversation started, a man might take over and ask you for your number or for a date. If he doesn't ask, however, it doesn't necessarily mean that he isn't interested. He might think that you are married, or he might think that it would be improper in such an unusual place as a bookstore, or he might just be afraid that you will say no. You have no idea what is going on in his head. You only know that if he doesn't ask you out, you need to ask him out if you want to see him again. At a bookstore, as in any other meeting situation, you have two closing options:

Close No. 1—Suggest an Activity and Give Him Your Number

Have a business card or pen and paper handy. Just hand him your number as you are leaving and say, "I have enjoyed talking with you. Give me a ring sometime if you'd like to continue our conversation." This low-pressure close is easiest for most women because there is no immediate rejection.

Close No. 2—Ask for a Date

When you directly ask for a date, it is not important what activity you suggest. The important thing is that you suggest *some* activity. If a man is interested in seeing you again, he will agree to almost any suggestion. You could ask for a date by saying:

"I have to go now. Would you like to meet for lunch some day next week?"

"I have enjoyed talking with you. Would you like to join me for a drink after work next week and continue our conversation?"

You don't have to talk to a man for a long time before you close. A ten- or twenty-minute conversation should be enough. By then you will probably know if you are interested in him.

Browsing is not the only way to meet a man in a bookstore. A friend of ours who is an avid reader told us that bookstore readings also offer possibilities for meeting men. Here is what she told us about readings:

I go to readings whenever I can. I enjoy them, and there are usually men there. One reading I went to had a large number of men because it was a reading of a new science book. I sat next to a cute guy and started a conversation by saying, "Do you enjoy this author's work?" We talked some before the speaker started. After the lecture, we continued our conversation. I told him about a lecture series on foreign affairs that I was coordinating. He seemed interested, so I gave him my number and said, "If you would like to attend one of our lectures, call me and I'll give you all the information." He called and asked about the next lecture, then he asked me out.

At first, the thought of going to a bookstore specifically to meet a man might seem ridiculous, or perhaps a bit scary. We know that it can be done, however, because we know women who have done it. Try it a few times and see what happens. Other women have met exciting and appealing men in bookstores. The men are there—it's just a matter of knowing how to meet them.

❦13❦

How to Meet a Man at a Singles Bar

Any bar might be considered a "singles bar" if it is a popular place for singles to meet. A singles bar could be a sports bar with a big-screen TV, a bar in a restaurant or hotel, or a bar with a dance floor and music provided by a disk jockey or live band. This chapter deals specifically with the type of bar where there is dancing. To get a date in the singles bars where there is no dancing, use the techniques given in chapter 10, "How to Meet a Man at a Singles Mixer."

You can call them singles bars, dance clubs, or night spots. No matter what you call them, they all have one thing in common: a bad reputation. There are classes for singles in "How to Avoid the Bar Scene." Personal ads in newspapers proclaim, "Hate the bar scene," or "Don't do bars." When a married couple who had first met in a singles bar were asked where they met, the woman replied, "We met at church." She obviously didn't want the stigma of a singles bar attached to her relationship.

A woman in our class said, "We all know what kind of people go to singles bars. You can't meet anyone nice there." Another woman said, "You know why men go to singles bars. They are there for only one reason." A woman who didn't mince words said, "When a man sees a woman in a singles bar, especially if she's alone, he thinks she's there just to get laid."

If we were to spend more than a few minutes discussing singles bars in our class, someone would usually get irritated and ask us to move on to another topic. These people had made up their minds that singles bars were not good places to get a date. They didn't even want to discuss it.

Are singles bars really that bad? We know a lot of women who met their husbands or boyfriends at singles bars and think they got a good catch. Valerie is one woman who had a good experience in a singles bar.

I was living in Texas last year when my marriage of fourteen years went on the rocks and I lost my job. It seemed like a good time to start over, so I moved to Taos, New Mexico, and got a job working at the ski resort. One evening as I was exploring the night life in Taos, I found this little country dance bar. I had hardly gotten settled at a table when a rugged-looking middle-aged man with a beard asked me to dance. I was a little apprehensive at first, but Kevin turned out to be such a nice man. He had been an independent oil man when his doctor told him he was killing himself working so hard. He sold his business and got enough money that he didn't have to work anymore. Six months ago I quit my job at the ski resort so I could travel with Kevin.

After her experience meeting Kevin in a bar, Valerie thinks bars are good places to meet men. If some women think bars are terrible places to meet men, and other women think they are good places, who's right? Like any other singles meeting place, singles bars have both advantages and disadvantages. It is up to you to decide what will work for you.

Advantages of Singles Bars

There are lots of men in singles bars who are single and looking; that's why they are there. You will probably have your choice of several singles bars, each providing an opportunity to see different men.

If you are on a campaign to find the right man—and a campaign is a good way to find the right man—singles bars, because they are open most nights, can fill many gaps in your activity schedule.

Tip: *If you would enjoy an evening in a singles bar when there are far more men than women, go when it snows or when a storm is threatening. When the weather turns bad, many women stay home. Men, on the other hand, are less likely to change their plans because of the weather. Thus, there are more men to choose from and less competition!*

Disadvantages of Singles Bars

Singles bars can be hazardous to your health. Nonsmokers may object to the amount of smoke that floats around in some singles bars. In some bars the music is so loud that not only is it hard to have a conversation, it can actually damage your hearing. A dark, noisy, unfamiliar bar full of strangers can be downright intimidating if you're not used to it.

Tip: *The noise level in a singles bar can be a serious health issue. One of our students said he stood near a wall-mounted speaker in a singles bar two years ago, and his ears have been ringing ever since. To protect your hearing, wear earplugs. When you are wearing ear plugs you can still hear when people talk to you. Earplugs will make your voice sound louder to you than it does to others, however, and at least initially, you may not speak loud enough to be heard.*

If you avoid singles bars because of their bad reputation, you will miss out on one of the common ways singles meet. In most singles bars you will find many men who are attractive and decent. They are there because they are trying to meet a woman and they don't know where else to go. Not every man you meet in a singles bar is someone you would want to date, but the same thing could be said of the men you meet at work, church, or anyplace else. It's up to you to select the right man, no matter where you are. Don't prejudge a man simply because he is in a singles bar. We have a rule that applies to singles bars: *Judge the person not the place.*

On any given night when you are sitting home alone watching television and wishing you had a male companion, there are nice guys in singles bars wishing they had a female companion. You won't meet these men sitting on your living room couch.

Getting Used to the Singles Bar Atmosphere

During a discussion of singles bars in one of our classes, we told the class that their chances of meeting someone would improve if they visited several different bars in one evening. A woman who was sitting next to her girlfriend said, "We went to seven different singles bars in one evening." At first we were impressed. Some women are intimidated by singles bars, but these two women didn't appear to be. The woman then added, however, "But we didn't go in any of them. We just peeked in the door. We were afraid to go in."

The fear these two women felt as they peeked in the door is not unusual. On their first trip to a singles bar, most women are apprehensive. They have heard about the bad reputation of bars and are expecting the worst. Many women who were initially apprehensive about singles bars, however, eventually start to enjoy them. We'll let Caroline describe her experience.

I hadn't had a date in two years, and finally decided I was going to have to get out of the house to meet men. I took a dance class hoping to meet someone there, but the only friend I made in the class was Brian. He was too old for me, but he was a good dancer and he helped me a lot in class. Brian suggested I try his favorite singles bar. He said people of all ages went there, and it was a good place to dance.

One Friday night I went to the bar Brian had recommended. When I walked in, I was overwhelmed. It was crowded and noisy, and so dark I could hardly see. I didn't take my coat off or look for a place to sit. I just stood there feeling panicky.

Brian was there, and when he saw me, he came over and asked what was wrong. I said, "I'm afraid. I don't like this place. I think I'm going to leave."

Brian assured me that many women are afraid and feel overwhelmed on their first visit to a singles bar. I calmed down somewhat when he said he thought we should dance a little before I left, because if we didn't practice the dance steps we had learned, we would forget them. After we had danced for a while, he showed me the best place to sit to get men to ask me to dance. He told me to sit there, cross my legs, and bounce my foot in time with the music to make it look as if I was full of energy and wanted to dance. Brian recommended I come back two more times before I passed judgment on the place.

I followed his advice and went back two more times. It got easier each time. I didn't have any bad experiences and the men I met were very polite. After the third time, I was used to the place and started to have fun. Never again will I sit home alone Friday or Saturday night wishing I had a boyfriend. When I go to a singles bar I have a chance to meet men, and I have fun dancing.

When you make your first trip to a singles bar, take the advice that Brian gave Caroline: Don't give in to your fear and leave. Stay for the evening, and then return at least two more times. It often takes that long to become comfortable in a new place, especially a dark, noisy bar full of strangers. It may be hard to believe now, but you may learn to enjoy the singles bar atmosphere and get to the point where you look forward to going.

HOW TO MAKE YOURSELF MORE APPROACHABLE IN A SINGLES BAR (THE PASSIVE TECHNIQUE)

Here's how to use the Passive Technique in a singles bar:

Be Alone

Men who know how to dance will ask you to dance even if you are with a group of friends. But what about the men who don't dance?

Most of them will be reluctant to approach you and start a conversation if you are with one or more friends. To have both the dancers and nondancers approach you, be alone.

Make Eye Contact and Smile

Many men won't approach a woman in a singles bar until they have made eye contact and received some kind of an encouraging signal from her. When you see a man you would like to meet, give him this encouragement—make eye contact and smile.

Don't Wear a Ring on Your Wedding-Ring Finger

In the dim light of a singles bar, a man can easily mistake an ordinary ring for a wedding ring. Don't wear *any* ring on your wedding-ring finger.

Be Both Visible and Accessible

A good location, one both visible and accessible, can increase your chances of meeting a man by ten times, maybe even a hundred times, over a bad location. The more visible you are, the easier it will be for men to see you. The more accessible you are, the easier you are to approach.

There are some locations where you will be highly visible, but so inaccessible that few men will approach you. For example, if there were tables on a balcony overlooking the dance floor and you were to sit at one of these tables in a chair next to the railing, you would be highly visible. To reach you, however, a man would have to climb the stairs (with everyone watching) and then squeeze past the people sitting in the other chairs to get near you at the railing. Only men experienced at meeting women will attempt such an approach.

Being near a high-traffic area is best, especially if you are sitting on a bar stool or standing. Not only will you be visible to men passing by, you will also be easily accessible to men who want to talk or ask you to dance. A location near the path to the dance floor is excellent. Another choice location is at the bar next to the service counter where men will come to order drinks. Here you will have a perfect opportunity to talk with each man as he waits alone for several minutes while the bartender prepares his drink.

Another good place to sit is on a bar stool at a railing next to the dance floor. In this location you will be visible to men on the dance floor and accessible if a man wants to ask you to dance. In a row of bar stools, choose the end stool where you will be more accessible. This end seat will increase your chances of being asked to dance and of having a man start a conversation.

Tip: *If you plan on sitting and want a good seat, get there early. The women regulars know where the good seats are, and often go early to be sure to get one.*

Sitting in a chair at a table is not as good as sitting on a bar stool or standing, but it's still okay as long as you are visible and easily accessible. You will still meet the men who dance, but usually not the men who just want to strike up a conversation.

Avoid places where you can't be easily seen or easily approached, such as a table in an inaccessible corner of the bar or where tables are jammed close together. It is hard to see you there, and because it draws attention to their approach, most men hate squeezing behind chairs to get near a woman. If you do sit at a table or booth, some seats should be avoided. As an example, let's look at the situation of five women sitting in a booth and analyze why some of the seats are bad places to sit.

FIVE WOMEN IN A BOOTH

It should be obvious that if all of the women shown in the drawing on the next page are equally attractive to a man, Mary and Liz have the best chance of being asked to dance, Jane and Beth have less chance, and Sandy has the lowest chance of all. In a noisy dance spot, a man must lean across the table in front of two women to talk to Jane, Sandy, or Beth. Men don't like to do this because it makes them feel as if they are rejecting these women in favor of their companion. In

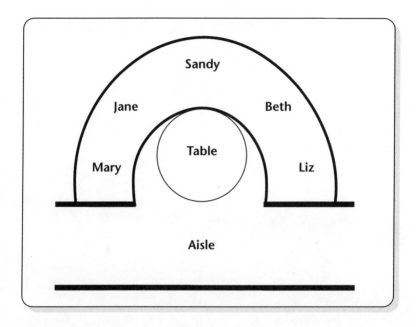

addition, they feel they will have an audience for their potential rejection. These bad locations limit you to meeting only the men who know how to dance and those who are experts at meeting women. Most of the men who want to start a casual conversation will be eliminated.

On the next page is a sample layout of a singles bar. It shows the desirability of the different locations, from best to worst.

These suggestions for making yourself more approachable will increase your chances of success in a singles bar. There is a way to be even more successful in a singles bar—use the Active Technique.

HOW TO USE THE FIVE STEPS IN A SINGLES BAR (THE ACTIVE TECHNIQUE)

In a singles bar (or anyplace else) it must be awful to have to wait passively for a man to approach, not knowing if you will like him and worrying about how to get rid of him if you don't. It's so much better to take control of the situation by selecting the men you will dance with and meet. The Active Technique gives you this control.

Where to Sit or Stand in a Singles Bar

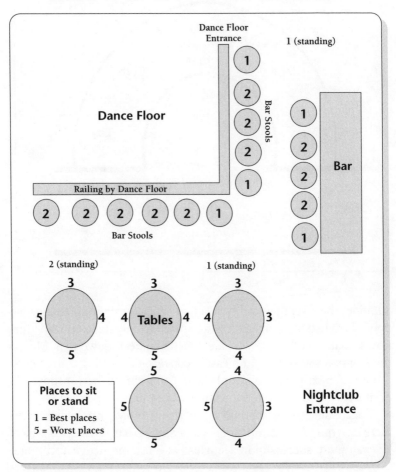

Step 1—Search

If you sit or stand in one spot, you will see the men nearby and the men passing by, but you won't see the men in other parts of the bar. To see these men, stand in one spot for few minutes, then move to another location and again casually take note of the men nearby.

Make several tours of the club. Don't give up. Keep searching, even if you think there is nobody there you would like to meet. In a busy singles bar people are constantly arriving and leaving, going in and out of the rest rooms and on and off the dance floor. You can easily miss someone if you only make one tour of a busy club. The most effective way to search is to continue to move from spot to spot until you see a man you would like to meet. Your second or third tour of the club might reveal a man who has just come in or who was hidden from view.

Be aware of men on the dance floor. If you see an interesting man, watch to see if he stays with his dance partner when the dance is over. If he leaves her, he's a good candidate to ask to dance because you know he can dance and probably isn't there with a date.

Your search in a singles bar is not like a search for a lost contact lens. It doesn't have to be that obvious. Just move from place to place and discreetly check out the men. In a singles bar most people are concerned with their own efforts to meet someone and won't notice or care what you are doing.

Step 2—Get Near

How you get near is determined by what the man is doing. If he is standing alone or sitting on a bar stool, you can easily get near by casually moving in beside him. There is usually a lot of moving about going on in a singles bar, and he will not find it unusual that you are suddenly standing there. When you stand close to a man, you have a good chance of meeting him. Even if you don't do any more of the Five Steps, he might take over and start a conversation or ask you to dance. You have made it easy for him by being nearby.

If the man is sitting at a table, or standing and having a conversation with a group of people, the easiest way to get near him is to combine Steps 2 and 3 by walking up to him and saying, "Would you like to dance?"

Step 3—Break the Ice

As mentioned, you can always break the ice with "Would you like to dance?" Few other meeting situations offer such an easy icebreaker. It's a common and always acceptable icebreaker that you can use to meet any man in the place.

If you don't want to dance, there are other options for icebreakers. You can use a planned icebreaker or a spontaneous icebreaker. Here are some planned icebreakers that you can always use:

"Do you like this song [band]?"

"What do you think of this place?"

"How are you tonight?"

"Hi, my name is Janie."

Tip: *An icebreaker to avoid is, "Do you come here often?" If he does, he might not want to admit it for fear of being labeled a bar lizard.*

For a spontaneous icebreaker, comment on the man's clothes, a couple who are especially good dancers, the weather, or almost anything else that comes to mind. For example:

"I like that tie. It looks good on you."

"Is it always this busy [dead] in here?"

"What time does happy hour end?"

"Don't they dance well together?"

What you say is not critical. The important thing is to just say something so the man will know you want to talk.

Tip: *If you ask a man to dance and get turned down, don't leave. Keep talking and see if you get positive feedback. Some men are insecure about their dancing ability and will turn down your offer to dance even though they would like to meet you.*

Step 4—Continue the Conversation

Now that you have broken the ice and started a conversation, you can spend a few minutes on small talk. Before long, however, focus on achieving your conversation goals.

Conversation Goal No. 1—Get Insurance

Get insurance (his name and enough information about where he works to enable you to reach him by phone) as soon as possible in a singles bar because there are many possibilities for interruptions. You might be dancing with a man, thinking you have plenty of time to learn more about him, when suddenly the disk jockey stops the music and announces karaoke, a limbo contest, or a name-that-tune contest. At this point the man, being uncomfortable, might return to his seat to be with his friends. Once separated, you might not have a chance to talk to him again. If you have insurance, you will have a second chance to talk to him.

Conversation Goal No. 2—Qualify Him

Find out if he meets your most important requirements before you agree to a date, or you might be wasting your time. Jennifer learned this lesson the hard way:

One night shortly after my divorce, I met a really great-looking guy at a dance spot. It was pretty obvious there was a strong mutual attraction. After we had talked and started to get to know one another, he asked me out for dinner the next evening. I spent all the next day in a dream world, fantasizing about him. But at dinner, I got some bad news. When I asked him to tell me about himself, he droned on and on about his work. Eventually I said, "You have just spent half an hour talking about your work. You haven't said a thing about your personal life. Tell me about *you!*" He was silent for a moment and wouldn't look at me. When I asked him what was wrong, he told me he was married. I was terribly disappointed. I liked him a lot and my hopes were pretty high. Ever since, before I make a date with a man, I find out if he is married. I just come right out and ask him. Somehow, it's not as awkward as I thought it would be.

Because some married men go to singles bars to try to get something going on the side, "Are you married?" could be an important question to ask. Also, some out-of-town businessmen enjoy spending their evenings on the road flirting with women in a singles bar. If you don't want to spend your evening entertaining a man who will be gone the next day, ask, "Where do you live?" or "Do you live around here?"

Avoid wasting a lot of time with a man who is not right for you. Qualify him early in the conversation. Then if you decide you are not interested, end the conversation and spend your time looking for someone who does meet your requirements.

Conversation Goal No. 3—Drop Hints

Even if you are bold enough to close, you still might prefer to have the man ask you out. You can encourage him to take the initiative by dropping hints. During the conversation, find an area of mutual interest and say how much you enjoy that activity. This might encourage him to ask for a date involving that activity. For example:

> "I can see why you enjoy golf. I'm taking lessons and really love the game. I just need more practice."

> "You work not too far from where I do. Have you found any good lunch places?"

You can also drop hints that let him know you like being with him. For example, you could say, "It's fun dancing with you. You have a good lead."

There are also nonverbal hints that let a man know you like him. One powerful clue you can give a man is to give his hand a little squeeze. You can do this while dancing, while waiting hand-in-hand for the next song, or when he takes you by the hand to lead you on or off the dance floor. You can also dance with him as long as he wants. This tells him you are interested.

Conversation Goal No. 4—Extend Your Time Together

Finding a way to extend your time together is not as important in a singles bar as in some other places. For example, if you met a man while walking in the park, a suggestion to get ice cream from a nearby vendor is a way to gradually make the move from a casual encounter to a romantic encounter. People go to singles bars with the intent of meeting someone and getting a date, however, and it's perfectly acceptable to ask for a date without first spending a great deal of time together. If you do feel you want to get to know the man better before committing to a date, you can extend your time together by inviting him to sit at your table, or you can suggest going out on the patio or to a quieter part of the bar where it will be easier to talk.

Tip: Before you invite a man to sit at your table, be fairly sure he is the only man you want to meet that evening. If a man accepts your invitation to sit at your table, he might be there for the rest of the evening. Getting him to leave could be awkward, and there is little chance other men will approach you while he is there.

Step 5—Close

If he hasn't closed, you might as well do it. It's the only way you can find out if he is a potential partner. You can use either of the two closing options.

Close No. 1—Suggest an Activity and Give Him Your Number

Suggest an activity the two of you could do together and give him your number. For example:

"I enjoy dancing with you. If you would like to go dancing again sometime, give me a call. Here's my work number."

"I enjoyed meeting you this evening. If you would like to get together for lunch sometime, give me a call. Here's my number."

Compared to saying nothing, this assertive behavior greatly increases your chances of getting a date.

Close No. 2—Ask Him for a Date

Here's what you might say in a singles bar:

"I enjoyed talking to you this evening. Would you like to continue this conversation over lunch next week?"

"The Volunteers for the Homeless are holding a charity dance next Saturday. It will be ballroom dancing to a live band. Would you like to go with me?"

Directly asking for a date may be the only way you will be able to get a date with a man who is shy, because his lack of confidence may keep him from calling you even if you give him your number. One man in our class said he had recently met a woman who gave him her number and asked him to call. When asked if he had called her yet, he replied, "No. I'm going to wait a couple of weeks. A woman that pretty must surely be busy." In two weeks he will probably say, "There's no use calling her now; she's probably forgotten about me."

Tip: When exchanging phone numbers with a man in a bar, ask for both his work and home numbers. If he seems reluctant to give you his home number, he's probably married or living with someone. If he does give you his home number, call him up to confirm your date (and to see who answers the phone).

Kim used the Active Technique to meet Andy in a western dance bar. Here's how their meeting looked from Andy's perspective.

After I broke up with my girlfriend, I started going to singles bars to try to meet someone. Chaps was within walking distance of my condo, so I went there a lot. One Friday I was circulating through the crowd at Chaps when I saw this woman with long, straight, dark hair and no makeup standing next to the dance floor. She didn't look like my type, so I decided not to ask her to dance.

About an hour later, after asking a dozen women to dance, dancing with four, and asking two for a date with no success, this dark-haired woman came over to me, looked up shyly and said, "Would you dance with me?" This was the first time a woman had ever asked me to dance. I was flattered, and automatically said, "Sure."

We introduced ourselves and talked while we danced. I started to find her interesting and attractive. We had a lot in common, and her soft voice and pretty smile were very appealing. Then Kim said she was starting a new job in a month and would be moving two hundred miles away. I was disappointed, and wondered how I could make a graceful exit. It didn't seem reasonable to make a date with a woman about to move so far away. But when she said, "Would you call me sometime?" I said, "Sure I'll call you. Give me your number." Again, this had never happened to me before.

I called her and we began dating. We continued to see each other after she moved away. The two hundred miles turned out to be an inconvenience, not an insurmountable problem.

The women Andy was asking to dance were those he was immediately attracted to because of their looks, a typical situation in singles bars (and almost everywhere else). Initially, Kim wasn't as attractive to Andy as many of the women were at Chaps that night, but she was able to get the man she wanted by using the Active Technique. After spending some time dancing with Kim, Andy started liking her enough to go out on a date. After dating for a short time, he was willing to travel two hundred miles to see the same woman he initially wouldn't ask to dance when she was standing two feet away.

This story of Kim using the Active Technique to meet Andy is true. We know of many other women who used this technique to meet their man. The Active Technique puts you in control and lets the man see the person you really are, not just your face and figure. When you ask a man to dance, don't be shy or apologetic about the fact that you have taken the initiative. You have every right to ask a man to dance. Just walk up to the man with a smile and say, "Would you like to dance?" Many times a man who won't ask you to dance will be happy to if you ask him. Once you are dancing, the man might decide he likes you because of your smile, voice, and personality.

JERK CONTROL

You will enjoy singles bars more after you learn how to handle the occasional pushy or obnoxious man you might meet there, the kind who give singles bars a bad name. You can learn to handle such men with a little practice, but you won't ever learn how if you are driven off by the first negative experience you have.

Melissa, a woman in our class, said she had only gone to a singles bar one time. According to Melissa, she had just walked in and was standing there looking at the dance floor when a man came up to her and said, "Let's go out on the dance floor and get each other excited." She left immediately and never went back, not there and not to any other singles bar. Her worst fears had been realized the first minute of her first visit.

This man probably had a few drinks in him and thought he was being funny. It wasn't funny to Melissa, though—she was frightened. It's unfortunate this incident occurred on her first visit. Women who frequently go to singles bars learn how to handle these situations. For example, Linda, a friend of ours, feels totally comfortable in singles bars, but it wasn't always that way. She told us what it was like on her first visit to a singles bar when a man sat at her table, uninvited.

The first time I went to a singles bar, a man walked me back to my table after a dance, sat down, and started talking to my girlfriend and me. I didn't like him and I didn't want him sitting there, but I didn't know how to get him to leave. I decided to try staying in the restroom for a long time, hoping he would get the hint and leave. My girlfriend and I stayed in the restroom for ten minutes, but when we came out, he was still there, so we went back and sat with him again.

When he asked me to dance again, I decided to try something else. As we were walking off the dance floor this time, I said to him, "I enjoyed dancing with you and I would like to dance with you again later, but right now I want to dance around a little while." That worked. He left and didn't bother me anymore.

I never have any trouble now that I have learned what to do. If a man asks me to dance and I don't want to, I simply say, "No, thank you." If I dance with a man and decide I don't want to dance with him again, at the end of a song I say, "Thank you!" and turn and walk off the floor. This "thank you" at the end of the song is a common signal that most men understand to mean, "I'm not interested in you." If a man asks if I would like to go out and I don't want to go, I say, "I don't think so, but thank you for asking." I don't think I owe a man an explanation of why not.

I've never had to do this, but if a man wouldn't leave me alone, I would tell the bouncer or bartender. Some of my girl-friends always sit at the bar because they feel more secure being near the bartender.

Linda no longer worries about how to say no or how to get rid of men. Her clear, simple, and direct actions put a quick end to potentially uncomfortable situations.

Tip: When you go to the same singles bar over a long period of time, you may become buddies with some of the men who are regulars. They will dance with you and ask you to sit at their table and talk, but they won't ask you out. Either you don't interest them romantically or they are not there to find someone to date. If you are there to find someone to date, limit the time you spend with the regulars. Remain free so you can move through the crowd to find someone new and so you will be available if a new man wants to ask you to dance.

Try different singles bars until you find one that has a clientele that suits you. Visit this bar until you get comfortable there, and then follow our suggestions for meeting men. Don't worry about the fact that you are meeting a man in a bar. Judge the person, not the place.

◈14◈

How to Meet a Man at a Running Event

*I*f you think a running event is an unusual place to try to meet a man, you are not alone. In one of our classes, when we recommended running events as a way singles could meet, one woman said, "You've got to be kidding. That's bizarre!" We know from experience, however, that it's not only possible, but in a way, romantic, to make contact in a "nonstandard" meeting situation such as a run. With some analysis and planning, you can easily meet men at running events, as well as at other athletic activities. Skiing, biking, hiking, tennis, racquetball and similar activities all have great potential, a potential that can be fully realized by learning how to make yourself more approachable and by learning how to apply the Five Steps at each event.

Running events have become "happenings" with large crowds, food, and entertainment. Hundreds, thousands, even tens of thousands of spectators and athletes show up for these celebrations of fitness. The good news for you? Men far outnumber the women, and it's easy to create meeting opportunities and talk to strangers in the relaxed atmosphere of a running event.

You don't have to be a well-conditioned athlete to meet a man at a run. Running events attract beginning joggers, competitive athletes, and all levels in between. If you are not a jogger, then volunteer to help put on the run. This gives you a reason to be there and puts you in contact with runners, spectators, and other volunteers.

Any run is a good place to meet a man, but the best runs are those that attract large numbers by targeting the general public. Newspapers, running-shoe stores, running clubs, and joggers can tell you the schedules and characteristics of runs in your area.

Tip: *Nearby runs are best. The farther from home you go, the less chance you have of meeting someone who lives close enough to date.*

Advantages of Meeting a Man at a Run

The biggest advantage is the predominance of active, health-conscious men. You won't find many couch potatoes or men with substance abuse problems at a run. If you are fitness- and health-conscious, you have a good chance of meeting a compatible man. In addition, a run provides a daytime activity with lots of people where you will feel safe meeting men.

Disadvantages of Meeting a Man at a Run

In places like shopping malls, health clubs, and singles bars you can meet men almost any day of the year. Runs, on the other hand, occur on a limited schedule, making them more of an infrequent "special event" meeting opportunity.

HOW TO MAKE YOURSELF MORE APPROACHABLE AT A RUN (THE PASSIVE TECHNIQUE)

If you wait to be approached, you have two strikes against you. One strike is the fact that at a run, most men are there for the event itself, and meeting women isn't on their minds. The second strike is the simple fact that a run is not your typical singles meeting place. Even if a man goes to a run with the thought of meeting someone, he probably lacks the nerve and skills to do so. Therefore, if you are going to be successful using the Passive Technique, you need to make yourself so approachable a man can't ignore the meeting opportunity in front of him. Here are some ideas you can use to awaken men to the possibility of approaching you.

Be Alone

When a man sees a woman who is with one or more people, he may wish that he could meet her, and that will be the end of it. When a man sees a woman who is alone, he's likely to think, "She's alone—perhaps she'd like some company." To make it easy for men to meet you, register for the run alone, run alone, and be alone after the run. You can drive there with a friend, but separate after you arrive.

Make Eye Contact and Smile

At a run many men will need a strong signal from you to give them the courage to approach. Eye contact with a smile is that signal.

Wear a Conversation Piece

Help a man think of something to say by wearing a flashy or unusual running outfit or a T-shirt with words or a picture he can comment on. A button with a saying, a piece of jewelry, or an unusual water bottle could also give him ideas for an opener.

Don't Use a Headset

A headset makes it difficult for men to talk to you. Leave yours at home.

HOW TO USE THE FIVE STEPS AT A RUN (THE ACTIVE TECHNIQUE)

Even if you make yourself approachable at a run, your chances of meeting a man with the Passive Technique still aren't good. Most of the men will have the run on their minds, and the few men who are hoping to meet a woman will rarely try. The Five-Step Active Technique is the best way for you to make something happen at a run. There are three distinct time periods at running events: before the run, during the run, and after the run. Each period presents unique meeting opportunities.

THE ACTIVE TECHNIQUE BEFORE A RUN

Because time is limited, it's not easy to complete all Five Steps before the run. Therefore, your objective before the run is to set the stage for continuing a conversation after the run. Do this by searching for a man to meet, starting a conversation, and then, when it's getting close to the start of the race, making an offer to meet again after the run.

Step 1—Search

Most runners will arrive within an hour of the start of the race. Arrive early, register, and be ready to search as the men arrive. That way, you have more time to search and more time to talk to a man.

> **Tip:** Watch the men as they arrive to see if they are in the company of a woman. Sometimes couples arrive together, but split up to register and run.

Step 2—Get Near

Before the race there are many opportunities for getting near any man you want to meet. The registration line, the water line, the general crowd milling around, or the mob assembling at the starting or finish line all provide opportunities to get near. Depending on the situation, you can get in line behind the man or casually move in next to him. If you spot an appealing man and can't find a way to get near, watch for opportunities during and after the race.

Step 3—Break the Ice

It's easy to start a conversation before a run. All you need to say to break the ice is something like, "Nice day, isn't it?" or "Have you done this race before?" Most men with a few minutes to kill before the race would be pleased to have someone to talk to.

Step 4—Continue the Conversation

There is a good chance your conversation will get interrupted by the start of the race or by the man wanting to stretch and get ready to run. Because of this looming interruption it is important that you achieve the conversation goals of getting insurance and extending your time together.

You can usually get insurance (his name and enough information about his work to call him there) in the first two or three minutes of a conversation. After getting insurance you can continue the conversation by asking qualifying questions. When an interruption occurs, suggest meeting again after the race. If you separate without making specific plans to meet later, you might never see him again. Be prepared to suggest meeting later. For example:

"The run is about to start. Would you like to meet at the finish and see how we did?"

"Would you like to watch the awards ceremony after the run? We could meet by the water table."

Step 5—Close

Before the run you probably won't have time to close or even be sure that you want to. That's why arranging to meet him after the run is important.

THE ACTIVE TECHNIQUE DURING A RUN

Step 1—Search

Check out the men running nearby.

Step 2—Get Near

Adjust your speed to get alongside the man you would like to meet.

Step 3—Break the Ice

When you are alongside the man, it's easy to say, "How's your run going?" When you make an opening remark to a stranger, note the tone in which he responds. It's an indication of his openness to some conversation. This especially applies when speaking to a man involved in an activity such as running a race where he may be trying to set his "personal best" time. If he responds positively, keep the conversation going. If it's a neutral response, try a few more remarks and see if he warms up. If it's negative, you may want to drop it with "Have a good run" and maybe try to meet him after the race.

Step 4—Continue the Conversation

Once you start talking, you might be able to continue talking until the race ends. If he does start to pull away, you could say, "Would you like to meet at the finish and get some refreshments?" Usually a man won't change his pace if he's interested in you, and you will have time to achieve your conversation goals.

Step 5—Close

Usually you'll need to wait until the end of the race to close, but if an opportunity comes up during the run, go ahead and close. For example, if he says he needs a running partner, volunteer and then offer to exchange numbers when you finish the race.

THE ACTIVE TECHNIQUE AFTER A RUN

The best time to do all Five Steps is after the run; however, there still is a time constraint. Although some people stay around after the run for refreshments and the awards ceremony, others start leaving immediately. This time constraint forces an effective execution of the Five Steps.

Step 1—Search

People will be milling about after the run, eating, drinking, and watching the awards ceremony while they recover from the run.

Walk around through the crowd or stand near a high-traffic area to see who is available. Don't limit your search to just the runners— remember the hundreds of spectators and volunteers. Couples get back together after the run, so unattached men are easy to spot.

Tip: *Plan on staying until most of the crowd is gone because this is a good time to spot a man who doesn't have a woman in his life. Married men and men with girlfriends often have obligations after the run and may not hang around. A man without a woman is more likely to linger and kill time.*

Step 2—Get Near

After you have found a man you want to meet, discreetly follow him until there's an opportunity to get near him. If he's at the water or refreshments table, stand next to him. If he's sitting on the grass, sit near him. If he's standing with some friends, stand near him.

Step 3—Start a Conversation

As always, having a few openers ready will increase your confidence. Here are some planned openers that you can use after a run:

"Did you have a good run?"

"How long have you been a jogger?"

"What was your time?"

"Have you done this run before?"

"Do you know if they are going to have an awards ceremony?"

Tip: *Many, if not most, men at a run will be wearing a T-shirt from a previous run. Because this is so common, one of your planned icebreakers could be a comment on his T-shirt such as, "The Cherry Blossom 10K—where's that run held?"*

You can also use a spontaneous icebreaker that fits a particular situation, such as:

"This is a big crowd. Does this run usually attract so many people?"

"That head wind was really something. Did it hurt your time?"

Step 4—Continue the Conversation

Because you never know how long a man is going to hang around after the run, when you get a conversation started, put special emphasis on the conversation goals of getting insurance and qualifying the man to determine if you would like to see him again.

Conversation Goal No. 1—Get Insurance

In the first few minutes of your conversation ask questions about his name and where he works so you could call him there if your conversation gets interrupted and you don't have an opportunity to close.

Conversation Goal No. 2—Qualify Him

Since a run is a nonsingles event, you may want to find out if he's involved. "Does your girlfriend run?" would work. If you qualify a man and find out he is not right for you, move on. You might still have time to meet someone else.

Conversation Goal No. 3—Drop Hints

As with all other places you might meet a man, dropping hints is an optional goal. If you want the man to ask you out, here's what you could say to help him get up the nerve:

"There's a 10K trail run next Sunday. I've been thinking of entering."

"I usually run after work, but running alone is getting boring."

"Have you hiked the Smoky Hill trail? I've heard it goes through some beautiful country."

Conversation Goal No. 4—Extend Your Time Together

Take a small but significant step towards a romantic relationship (and find out if he is interested in you) by suggesting something like:

"Would you like to join me in a walk around the lake?"

"I'm getting lunch at the Sub Shop on Fourteenth Street. Would you like to join me?"

If you get a positive response, he's probably available and interested. If he says "No, thanks," don't give up and walk away. Give it one more parting shot. Go on to Step 5 and close by saying, "Would you like to get together another time?" That way you'll find out for sure whether he's interested.

Step 5—Close

If you are about to separate and he hasn't asked for a date, it's time for you to take the initiative. Use either closing method:

Close No. 1—Suggest an Activity and Give Him Your Number

For example, you could say:

"It's been nice talking with you. If you would like to go jogging sometime, give me a ring. Let me borrow a pencil and I'll write down my number on your racing bib."

"I have to go now. If you'd like to continue our conversation over lunch sometime, I work for Capitol Finance. I'm the only Carol in the office. I'd like to hear from you."

"If you're interested in going on a bike ride, call me. I'm the J. J. Foster in the phone book."

Close No. 2—Ask for a Date

Here are some examples of this effective closing method:

"I have to go now. Would you like to get together for lunch next week?"

"It's supposed to be a nice day tomorrow. Would you like to go for a bike ride?"

"Would you like to go jogging together sometime?"

You can also suggest an immediate date, such as:

"I'm going for a bike ride this afternoon. Would you like to join me?"

If he accepts your offer of a date, be sure to get his phone number.

For the most part, men go to a run for the sake of the run, not to meet a woman. A lot of these men don't get out on the singles scene much and aren't used to approaching women. If you meet one of these men by doing the Five Steps, he'll never know this "chance" meeting was a planned effort on your part. He'll think he just got lucky.

≈Epilogue≈
It's Time to Get Started

We were at a party recently where Peggy, a single woman who had just learned that we teach a class on how to get a date, told the following story about an encounter she had in a pet food store:

This attractive man behind me in the check-out line had two huge bags of dog food and a huge bag of cat food. I wanted to meet him, so I said, "You must have a lot of dogs and cats, do you live on a farm?" He laughed and said, "I don't live on a farm, but I do have a house in the country on ten acres. I have three dogs and five cats. They are great companions. The only problem I have is when I travel on business I have a hard time finding someone to take care of them while I'm away."

From what he said about needing someone to take care of his animals I got the impression that he was single. I wanted to go out with him, but I didn't know how to make it happen. It occurred to me that I could ask him where he worked—that seemed like the logical next question after he said he traveled a lot on business, but somehow that seemed like too personal a question to ask. The conversation died when it was my turn at the cash register. I would really have liked to have gone out with him. What could I have done differently?

We told Peggy that she might have been able to get a date in the pet food store by giving the man her card and saying, "I would like to talk with you again. If you want to continue this conversation over lunch sometime, just give me a call."

We also told Peggy that she had to quit worrying about what other people think because it was getting in the way of her meeting Mr. Right. If she had asked the man in the store where he worked, rather than thinking her question was "too personal," he would probably have been pleased that she was interested in him, and he would have certainly answered her question. She then might have had enough information to call him at a later time.

Worrying that a question is "too personal," or because you heard that men don't like aggressive women, or because your mother said, "Don't you dare ask a man for a date," or because someone may be watching as you approach a man and know what you are doing— all of this gets in the way of your doing what you should do. Once you get to the point where you can do what you need to do without worrying about what other people think, you will be well on your way to meeting the Right Man. It's time to get started.

A NOTE ABOUT OUR COMPANION BOOK, HOW TO MEET THE RIGHT WOMAN

When we started teaching classes on how to get a date, we taught separate classes for men and women. After we combined the classes into one class for both men and women, we could see how fascinated the students were to hear the point of view of the opposite sex and to learn about the problems they were having getting dates. If you would like to gain a valuable insight into the man's perspective on the subject of how to get a date, we recommend that you read *How to Meet the Right Woman* (Birch Lane Press).

Appendix A
Forms

The Type of Man I Want to Meet	
Category	**My Requirements**
Age	
Marital History	
Children	
Religion	
Geographic	
Smoking	
Drinking	
Drug Use	
Education	
Occupation	
Financial Status	
Character	
Type of Relationship	
Interests	
Other	

Where I Will Go

(Use Your Requirements as a Guide)
(Y = Yes, N = No, M = Maybe)

Places, Activities, & Organizations	Y	N	M
Adult enrichment classes			
Aerobics classes			
Amusement parks			
Apartment bldg. pools & rec rooms			
Art museums			
Ballroom dance clubs			
Beaches			
Bicycle group tours			
Bicycling clubs			
Bike paths			
Block parties			
Book discussion groups			
Bookstores with reading areas			
Botanical gardens			
Bowling leagues			
Bus tours			
Camping clubs			
Charities			

Places, Activities, & Organizations	Y	N	M
Charity and fund-raising events			
City parks			
City streets (busy areas)			
Civic groups			
Coffeehouses for sitting and reading			
Computer user groups			
Conservation organizations			
Country and Western dance clubs			
Country clubs			
Cross-country ski races			
Cruises			
Dance spots			
Dog owners and breeders clubs			
Dog shows			
Downtown celebrations			
Environmental groups			
Equestrian clubs			
Ethnic clubs			
Festivals (music, beer, seasonal, etc.)			
Folk dancing clubs			
Food courts			

Places, Activities, & Organizations	Y	N	M
Foreign language clubs			
Gambling casinos			
Gardening clubs			
Golf courses			
Health clubs			
Hiking			
Historical museums			
Historical societies			
Homeowners associations			
Horse races			
Ice rinks			
I.Q. clubs			
Lectures			
Libraries			
Motorcycle clubs			
Natural history museums			
Outdoor adventure tours			
Outdoor clubs			
Overweight singles clubs			
Parent organizations			
Parent/school organizations			

Places, Activities, & Organizations	Y	N	M
Parties			
Playgrounds			
Poetry reading clubs			
Political organizations			
Professional clubs of various types			
Professional singles clubs			
Public speaking clubs			
Recreational vehicle clubs			
Recreation centers			
Religious organizations			
Resorts			
Roller skating rinks			
Runs and triathalons			
Sailing clubs			
Self-help and therapy groups			
Shopping malls			
Single parents clubs			
Singles bars			
Singles support groups			
Ski clubs			
Ski resorts			

Places, Activities, & Organizations	Y	N	M
Soccer clubs			
Social mixers			
Softball teams			
Swimming clubs			
Tall clubs			
Tennis clubs			
Theater groups			
Touch football teams			
Travel clubs			
Volunteer organizations			
Widows and widowers clubs			
Zoos			
Other:			
Other:			
Other:			
Other:			
Other:			
Other:			
Other:			
Other:			
Other:			

Appendix B
Wallet Reminder Cards

The Five Steps of the Active Technique

1. Search (find someone you want to meet).
2. Get near (near enough to speak).
3. Break the ice (start a conversation).
4. Continue the conversation (four goals).
5. Close (arrange to see him again).
   • Suggest activity and give phone number.
   • Ask for a date.

Conversation Goals

1. Get insurance (enough information to reach him at work).
2. Qualify (does he meet your requirements?)
3. Drop hints that you like him or enjoy a certain activity.
4. Extend your time together (suggest going somewhere else right now).

My Planned Icebreakers

1. _____
2. _____
3. _____
4. _____
5. _____

Questions or Conversation Topics to Qualify a Man

1. _____
2. _____
3. _____
4. _____
5. _____

How to Make Yourself More Approachable

Be alone.

Be visible.

Be accessible (usually stand).

Make eye contact and smile.

Wear or carry a conversation piece.

Do not wear a ring on your wedding-ring finger.

Do not wear a stereo headset.

Make a Safe Date

- Limit his ability to reach you.
- Meet in a public place during daytime.
- Make a date with a time limit (e.g., breakfast, lunch, drinks after work).
- Get his work phone *and* home phone.
- Obtain and verify information about him.

How to Get Better

Plan *each step before you go out.*
Practice *in your daily life:*
1. Searching.
2. Getting near.
3. Breaking the ice (habitually speak to strangers regardless of romantic interest).
4. Continuing the conversation (practice getting insurance and qualifying).

Where to Go

- Any place may have compatible people.
- Judge the person, not the place.
- Singles places have more singles, but also more competition.
- Nonsingles places probably have fewer singles and less competition.

Meet More People in Your Daily Life

As you go about your daily tasks:

- Actively look for opportunities.
- Vary when and where you go (e.g., eat at a different place or time).
- Think of icebreakers on the way.

Appendix C
Ideas for a First Date

With luck the man you are talking with will ask you for a date, but if he doesn't, you do have the option of asking him out or giving him your number and suggesting an activity. What you suggest usually is not critical. You don't have to be creative; a suggestion for lunch is always good. But if you want to be a little creative, here are some places and activities you could suggest for a first date:

Afternoon teas: At an English restaurant or traditional hotel.
Antique shops: Browse for the afternoon or for an hour before dinner.
Art galleries: Wander through several and comment on what you like and don't like.
Arts and crafts shows: Relaxing, interesting, and maybe educational.
Auctions: Estates, antiques, car, horse . . . Use your imagination; check the paper.
Badminton: Have a few games together; you can have fun without a great deal of skill.
Beer festivals: There are lots of new microbrews to try these days.
Bicycle rides: Ride to breakfast or lunch, have a picnic, or just a ride with conversation.
Boat rides: Rowboat, canoe, sailboat, whatever is available.
Bookstores: New or used; spend a couple of hours browsing together.
Bowling: Get close with a few gutterballs.
Breakfast: Go before work or have a leisurely meal on a weekend day.

Cards: Invite him for a game at your place or in a coffeehouse.

Carnivals: Be a kid again; win a stuffed animal, check out the rides, and eat some cotton candy.

Caving: Spelunk together.

Classes: Take a course that is of interest to both of you; have dessert afterward.

Coffeehouses: Have a little dessert and coffee. Great for people-watching and conversation.

Concerts: In a hall or arena, or in a park; classical, rock, or whatever suits you both.

Costume stores: This is a bit weird, but those who try it like it. Try a few costumes on for the fun of it. It may bring out the theatrical in you.

Country drives: Enjoy the scenery and explore a small town together.

Croquet: A nice, old-fashioned game followed by some lemonade—relaxing!

Dancing: Any kind you both like (if he doesn't dance, suggest taking lessons together).

Discussion groups: Books, current events, environmental, political.

Dog shows (or cat shows): These can be fun and different.

Entertainment: Check the entertainment section of your newspaper for music, comedians, plays, performance dance.

Errands: Need to pick out a new TV? Ask him along, then have dinner together.

Ethnic dining: Ethiopian, Thai, Chinese, Korean, Japanese, Greek, Italian—pick a cuisine you both like or one neither of you have tried before.

Exercise: Pump iron, aerobicize, or jog together, then have a health drink or dinner afterward.

Explore: Visit unfamiliar areas of town, drive twenty miles to a restaurant, visit new malls.

Fairs: County fairs, state fairs, medieval fairs, etc., are all good for wandering and people-watching.

Fishing: If you both like it, why not? If one of you hasn't tried it, get introduced to it. If neither of you has tried it, double the fun.

Frisbee: Go to the park and throw one around for an afternoon.

Gambling: If there is a casino nearby, try it out.

Games: Scrabble, chess, or checkers by a cozy fire can be romantic.

Garage sales: Spend a Saturday morning looking for treasure.

Golf: Eighteen holes or miniature can both be fun.

Grocery stores: Try a foreign or specialty store (some serve coffee or food).

Hike: After work with a picnic dinner or on a weekend.

Hobbies: Share one of your interests by visiting a hobby store (cooking, wine making, models, pottery).

Horseback riding: Western or English can make for a memorable afternoon.

Humor: Go to a comedy club, watch a comedy channel on cable, read a humor book together.

Ice skating: If the season is right or there is an inside rink, skate together for an evening or afternoon.

In-line skating: If you don't have skates, rent some and wobble around together.

Jigsaw puzzles: Or, if you prefer, crossword puzzles; both can be nice couples activities.

Lectures: Watch the paper for listings; outdoor equipment stores, travel agents, museums, zoos, business groups, and other places may give presentations and slide shows as well.

Libraries: Browse through the stacks and read periodicals or books.

Lunch: Take a break from work and rendezvous.

Movies: Try some you both like, or that one of you likes, or that neither of you likes.

Museums: Natural history, local, art. Try a variety, go to a special showing.

Musical entertainment: Jazz, folk, punk, classical—whatever the two of you like.

Picnic: After work or on a weekend afternoon; this can be a nice change from eating out.

Ping-Pong: If your clubhouse has a table, use it.

Play music: If one of you plays an instrument, entertain the other. If both of you play, have a duet.

Plays: Attend a show together, have coffee afterwards to discuss it.

Pool: There are lots of pool halls around.

Pub crawls: Brew pubs are gaining in popularity; try the ones in your town.

Races: Dogs, horses, or cars; take your choice.

Racquetball: Does your local parks and recreation or health club have a court?

Roller skating: Most cities have roller rinks. Give it a try.

Seminars: Choose a subject that interests both of you, and you will have something to talk about.

Skiing: If the season is right.

Spectator sports: Baseball, basketball, football, hockey; high school, amateur, or professional. Something to watch while you carry on a conversation.

Tennis: There are usually public courts around if you need one.

Tours: Be a tourist in your hometown. Visit historical sites and sites of interest.

TV: Watch your favorite program together.

Walk: A simple walk in the park can be relaxing and a nice way to communicate.

Wine tastings: Sampling different kinds of wine can make it a memorable evening.

Appendix D
A Sampling of Places to Go and Things to Do

Looking through an entertainment weekly paper, a daily paper, an adult enrichment class catalog, and the yellow pages, we found a multitude of places to go and things to do. Here is what we found in each of the four sources of information:

AN ENTERTAINMENT WEEKLY

In one of the entertainment weeklies that is popular in our area we found the following places to go:

Music and Concerts: 67 musical events, including a free Beethoven sonata concert at a college.

Theater: 45 theater events. One event that sounded interesting was an audience-participation improvisational comedy.

Film: 14 films at college campuses, museums, and auditoriums. Everything from movie classics to travelogues.

Sports and Recreation: 25 events. The coed volleyball game and the lectures on outdoor adventures sounded like they would be easy places at which to socialize.

Dance Performances: 3 events.

Politics: 6 events, including a panel discussion at a university on the subject of international sanctions.

Lectures and Workshops: 57 events, including a lecture for singles sponsored by a church and a museum lecture on endangered species.

Classes and Discussion Groups: 76 events, many for singles, including a class on conversation skills, a book discussion group, and several singles support groups.

Museums: 54 listed, including a motorcycle museum.

Auditions: 4 singing and acting auditions.

Volunteers: 47 groups listed that were requesting volunteers. Examples: tutoring adults in reading, ushering at a play, and assisting the homeless and the disabled.

Galleries: 67 listed, some with one-time showings, others with continuous exhibitions.

Kid's Stuff: 18 events and classes that give single moms a way to entertain the kids (and maybe meet a single dad).

Clubs: 125 commercial establishments, many with dance floors, offering rock, jazz, folk, country music, and jam sessions.

DAILY NEWSPAPER

In the weekend section of our paper we found the following places to go:

Concerts: 35 listed.

Theaters: 38 listed.

Children's Activities: 21 listed, including a watercolor class, story time at a library, and several events at museums.

Nature: 6 activities, several suitable for children.

Events: 28 listed, many great for socializing, including a book discussion group, a travel slide show, international folk dancing, line dancing, and an art festival.

Nightlife: 51 listings, mostly singles dance spots, various kinds of musical entertainment, and several comedy clubs.

Arts: 112 public and private art galleries and exhibits of painting, photography, ceramics, and pottery.

Dances: 33 listed, many for singles, including square dancing and ballroom, Latin, and folk dancing. The dances are sponsored by various organizations, including churches and dance studios.

Singles Events and Meetings: 37 listed, including ski trips, wind surfing outings, golf, and tennis.

ADULT SCHOOL CATALOG

The latest catalog we saw listed 352 classes, including:

Foreign Language: 23 classes.

Travel: 8 classes on in-state, national, and international travel.

Careers, Business, and Marketing: 64 classes. Everything from running a small business to multilevel marketing.

Communication: 6 classes on public speaking, and one on "the art of small talk" that might be a good place to meet a single man.

Personal Productivity: 8 time management classes.

Computer Skills: 12 classes.

Special Events: 16 events, including seminars on making yourself feel good, sex and relationships, and how to defuse verbal conflict.

Investing: 8 classes. Everything from the basics to advanced strategies.

Real Estate: 6 classes on how to buy a home.

Home Design and Gardening: 15 classes.

Art: 19 classes.

Writing: 16 classes on writing and how to get published.

Music: 9 classes and events, including several that would be great for meeting a man, such as opera outings, a class called "Brunch and the Symphony," and another called "Wine Tasting and Classical Music."

Acting: 8 classes.

Photography: 9 classes.

Anthropology: 4 classes.

Cooking, Beer Making, and Wine Tasting: 11 classes that would be especially good for socializing.

Social Dancing: 6 classes that are great for meeting men.

Around Town: 5 events where you go in a group to explore unique bars, cemeteries, and historical sights in the local metro area. These are hard to beat for meeting a man.

Connections: 7 classes that are meant for singles, including classes on conversation skills, flirting, making impressions, places to go, and discussion groups.

Relationships: 8 classes on relationship issues. Some just for singles.

Mind Works: 15 classes addressing hypnosis, handwriting analysis, miracles, and angels.

Yoga and Meditation: 18 classes.

Health and Massage: 14 classes on subjects such as burning fat, healing herbs, and sensual massage.

Growth: 5 classes on self-esteem and taking control of your life.

Outdoors and Sports: 16 classes that would be good for socializing, including classes on learning:

Tennis
Rock climbing
Fishing
Volleyball
Cycling
Kayaking
Horsemanship
Hiking
Golf
Snowshoeing

Yellow Pages

It is helpful to know the headings to look under. Here were some useful headings we found in our yellow pages.

Bands and Orchestras: 41 listed, everything from Philharmonic to Polynesian.

Bicycle Tours: 19 listed, mostly commercial tours.

Books: 278 bookstores listed.

Business and Trade Organizations: 56 listed. You might find one for your profession or industry.

Charities: 16 listed (call to see if they need volunteers).

Churches: Over 200 listed. Everything from Buddhist to Baptist. Many have singles activities and organizations.

Clubs: 122 listed. Some, such as hiking clubs, tennis clubs, tall clubs, bicycle clubs, and dating services, provide a good opportunity for meeting a man.

Coffee Shops and Coffeehouses: 77 listed, including some in combination with bookstores. Many coffeehouses have a relaxed "sit and socialize" atmosphere, and some feature musical entertainment and poetry.

Dance Instruction: 157 studios, many catering to singles. Taking group lessons will put you in contact (literally) with many single men.

Dating Services: 43 listed. If you can afford them, they can help you meet a man.

Gourmet Shops and Food Services: 44 specialty food shops and grocery stores, many with places where you can eat, drink coffee, and strike up conversations with the men around you.

Health Clubs: 96 listings of commercial establishments. If you know what to do, they can be great places to meet a man.

Historic Places: 4 listed. Volunteer to work at one of these places and you could meet a lot of men in one day.

Libraries—Public: 9 listed. Spend a lazy Saturday afternoon in a library, and use the Five Steps to meet a man who enjoys books.

Museums: 83 listed. Everything from Arabian horses to steam engines.

Professional Organizations: 35 listed.

Recreation Centers: 54 listed. Mostly city parks and recreation centers that offer inexpensive workout rooms, swimming pools, racquetball courts, golf, and various classes and instruction.

Restaurants: Hundreds listed, but only look for salad bar and cafeteria style restaurants where you can choose where to sit (so you can sit near a man who is alone).

Schools—Academic—Colleges and Universities: Dozens listed, many offering evening classes for adults.

Shopping Centers and Malls: Dozens listed. Those with food courts provide especially good opportunities for meeting a man.

Singles Organizations: 9 listed, mainly "for profit" introduction services. You might try one of these, if the price is right.

Skating Rinks: 13 ice and roller rinks listed.

Social Service Organizations: 248 listed.

Swimming Pools—Public: 23 listed.

Synagogues: 17 listed. Some have singles groups.